Women in Ministry

L.E. Maxwell
with Ruth C. Dearing

D1310586

Christian Publications
Camp Hill, Pennsylvania

Christian Publications
3825 Hartzdale Dr, Camp Hill, PA 17011

Faithful, biblical publishing since 1883

ISBN: 0-87509-587-9
©Copyright 1987 Ruth C. Dearing
Printed in the United States of America

95 96 97 98 99   5 4 3 2 1

Unless otherwise indicated, Scripture taken from the
HOLY BIBLE
AUTHORIZED KING JAMES VERSION

Cover Design by
Robert A. Baddorf

Contents

Publisher's Preface

One of L.E. Maxwell's enduring contributions to the evangelical world is undoubtedly *Women in Ministry*.

Written before the "politically correct" era, it contains a surprising view, particularly when one considers its context. L. E. Maxwell was an intensely conservative man, both in theology and practice, and he lived a life of service and sacrifice.

Maxwell's earlier books, *Born Crucified* and *Crowded to Christ*, summarize well his life's focus. *Women in Ministry* is not unlike the first two. Its passion also is freedom in Christ—a lifelong theme of L.E. Maxwell.

"L.E.," as he was affectionately known, was the only graduate of a Kansas Bible school now long forgotten. His mentor at the school was W.C. Stevens who came from the Missionary Training Institute at Nyack, New York and later went to Simpson Bible Institute in Seattle.

Maxwell went on to the prairies of Western Canada where he founded the Prairie Bible Institute, famous worldwide for its missionary fervor—and its rigorous rules of conduct.

From such a context, Maxwell addresses a theme that is as current as tomorrow—and surprisingly helpful.

K. Neill Foster, Publisher
January 1995

Foreword

Leslie E. Maxwell (1895–1984) was a man ahead of his times.

That comes as a surprise to some who have a superficial acquaintance with the Bible Institute he founded in 1922 with Fergus Kirk, dedicated Christian farmer living in the Three Hills district. But Prairie Bible Institute has been a continuing testimony to the courage, independence, and integrity of its founder in various ways.

For the last few years we have heard the insistence of some on the necessity of a simple lifestyle. Mr. Maxwell embraced such for himself and for the school right from the beginning. Living in a modest wood-framed building and forfeiting the possession of a car, his life was a model of the proper use of material things.

Dr. Ralph Winter, student at Prairie in 1950, has made the expression "the hidden peoples" popular among evangelicals and their cause pressing. Throughout his career Mr. Maxwell made sure in his teaching, preaching, and writing that the challenge of these hidden peoples was constantly emphasized.

In the area of Bible study a fresh emphasis is currently

being placed on inductive Bible study. This basic approach to the interpretation of the Scriptures Mr. Maxwell had learned from his own highly esteemed Bible teacher, W.C. Stevens, founder of the short-lived Midland Bible Institute of Kansas City. Mr Maxwell incorporated the principles of inductive Bible study into the basic Bible curriculum at Prairie and consistently warned his students against bringing interpretational prejudices or preconceived doctrinal positions to the study of the text of God's Word.

Finally in the area of the ministry of Christian women— which is the subject of this posthumously published book, carefully prepared from his notes by Miss Ruth C. Dearing— Mr. Maxwell was years ahead of those contemporary leaders who are seeking a rethinking of this whole issue on the part of evangelicals. Again influenced by W.C. Stevens, and through him by A.B. Simpson, founder of the Christian and Missionary Alliance, Mr. Maxwell actively promoted gifted women in the ministry of Prairie Bible Institute. Miss Dorothy Ruth Miller, author of what was for many years a standard textbook in Bible colleges—namely, *Ancient History in Bible Light*—was a ten-talent Christian leader of stately Victorian appearance. At Mr. Maxwell's request she often preached to the congregation in Sunday services.

Miss Ruth Dearing herself has served on the Board of Directors of the Institute, was frequently consulted by Mr. Maxwell when important decisions affecting the direction of the Institute were in the balance, was Principal of Prairie High School for 18 years, and taught Bible to classes of women and men in the Bible college division for many years.

In the world mission conferences of the Institute Mr. Maxwell willingly sat at the feet of some of the most dynamic speakers ever heard at Prairie—Miss Mary Morrison (now Mrs. Colin Peckham of Edinburgh, Scotland), Miss Gladys Aylward, known as the Small Woman, and Dr. Helen Roseveare.

Thus for Mr. Maxwell the ministry of women, not only on the field overseas but at home, was not only theoretically possible; he saw to it that it was actually permitted in the work of Prairie Bible Institute.

It is fair to say that when asked about the ordination of women Mr. Maxwell would stop short of making a case for such recognition. I would tease him at times, pointing out that the principles of exegesis employed by him to grant women freedom in Christ to minister the Word and to maintain positions of responsibility in the Institute would inevitably lead him to grant ordination to capable women. But at that point he would smile and shake his head, indicating his disagreement.

It was my privilege to work very closely with Mr. Maxwell for many years. We often shared quotations from the books we were reading. Recently I came across a poem that I am sure I would have read to him, and he would have responded appreciatively. Here it is:

> We men, we are the stronger sex—
>   It always has been so!
> We send our gifts to mission fields
>   To which the women go!
>
> While up the steepest jungle paths,
>   A woman bravely treads,
> We men who are the stronger sex,
>   Just pray beside our beds.
>
> While women leave to go abroad
>   The heathen souls to reach,
> We men, who are the stronger sex,
>   Just stay at home and preach.
>
> While women in some far off shack
>   Do brave the flies and heat,
> We men, who are the stronger sex,
>   In cool and comfort eat.

Fatigued and weary, needing rest,
 The women battle on,
We men, who are the stronger sex,
 Just write and cheer them on.

O valiant men—come let us sleep
 And rest our weary heads,
We shall not be the stronger sex
 If we neglect our beds! [1]

One further word. Readers will note that Mr Maxwell does not quote from recent literature. Most of his sources go back twenty years or more. There is an explanation for this. Mr. Maxwell had learned to cope with very poor eyesight. He had surgery for both cataracts and detached retinas. He courageously kept on teaching with ever poorer vision. This did not allow him to engage in much reading other than that necessary for his classes. I am sure that if he had been able he would have devoured the books now coming from the press in such abundance.

Ted S. Rendall
President
Prairie Bible Institute

1. Author unknown. The poem appears in Vernon J. Gosden, *All the Power You Need* (London: JEB Books, 1977), p. 39.

Introduction

For many years Mr. Maxwell had on his heart the urge to prepare a treatise on the ministry of women. His desire was that women might be set free from what he felt were unscriptural restrictions placed on them by many churches and Christian leaders; his only fear was that he might appear to endorse the "women's lib" movement which was then coming to the fore.

He had already collected material on the subject when his health began to fail. Realizing he could no longer continue, in March of 1982 he asked if I would undertake the completion of the book. Suggesting that I would be the coauthor, he gave me liberty to add, omit, and change anything he had written. I agreed to attempt it but told him that it was *his* book, not *mine*.

With a full teaching schedule, I found my time on the book was very limited. In September of 1983, however, I was able to put into his hands about two-thirds of the manuscript. Mr. Maxwell listened as Mrs. Maxwell read the manuscript to him, and he gave his endorsement. But in February of 1984 before the final chapters had been completed, he was called home.

My aim has been to present the material as nearly as possible in the way Mr. Maxwell had prepared it. The work represents the cream of his study and thinking over a considerable period of time. Many of his illustrations are drawn from Christian classics, such as *The Maréchale* and works of Madame Guyon, Mrs. Penn-Lewis, and others. Since Mr. Maxwell often talked with me about his concern for women in Christian ministry and at various times had read to me what he and others had written, I believe I understand his thinking about the whole issue and trust I have communicated this in the finished product. I have sought to document all of the quotations, but where unable to do so have so stated.

Let me give credit to my sister Kathleen, who has read and reread the material and has done considerable editing, and to Dr. T.S. Rendall for reading the manuscript and giving valuable suggestions. Finally, I would like to bear testimony to the fact that Mr. Maxwell's broad view of women's ministry has made possible for me a far wider field of service than I had dreamed possible.

His conviction that women should not be barred from public ministry stemmed partly from his admiration for and confidence in Miss Dorothy Ruth Miller, who had been his teacher in Bible school in Kansas City and his associate teacher at Prairie Bible Institute for fifteen years. Miss Miller's capable and Spirit-filled ministry both in the classroom and in the pulpit together with his own careful study and exegesis of God's Word brought Mr. Maxwell to the convictions you will find set forth in these pages.

Ruth C. Dearing
May 1985

Author's Preface

In this book we are seeking to justify women's privilege and liberty to participate in public Christian ministry. Over the years the writer along with his fellow-workers at Prairie Bible Institute has been engaged in the training of women as well as men for public ministry. These studies have been prepared with the single desire to bring blessing and encouragement to women, young and old, and direction to the Christian public.

We make no claim to exhaustive research or high scholarship, nor do we make any pretence to great literary or exegetical value in connection with the subject at hand. Our prayer is that *Women in Ministry* may prove of practical value in the lives of godly women who long to be free from bondage and fruitful in the service of their Lord and Master.

In attempting the final revision of the manuscript for publication, we are reminded of an old scholar's remark which seems forcibly verified, that "one half of man's life is too little to write a book—the other half too little to correct it when it is written."

It would be the sheerest ingratitude if I did not acknowledge the much able secretarial help given the author in order to put these thoughts together. Apart from this valuable service, this book could never have come into being.

L.E. Maxwell
March 1982

To the many young women
trained at Prairie Bible Institute
who have given their lives to the
proclaiming of the Gospel throughout
the world.

"The Lord giveth the Word;
the women that publish the tidings
are a great host."
Psalm 68:11, ASV

Chapter One

WHAT DOES THE SCRIPTURE SAY?

D oes Scripture permit women to exercise any audible public ministry in connection with the activities of the church today? Does Scripture have the answer to this important question of women's ministry?

The present era has been designated *woman's century.* "Civilized women, the world over, are aspiring to co-equal recognition with man in all departments of activity, and the point for Christians to answer is: What Scripture sanction is there for all of this?"[1] Yes, the crucial question is *what does the Scripture say?* Does God's Word sanction a woman's liberty to teach, preach, and minister in a public way? Inasmuch as we claim to make the Bible our sole rule of faith and practice, we must discuss our subject from the standpoint of God's eternal Word.

As an image-bearer for her Master, woman's complete equality with man is evidenced throughout the Word of God. In writing to the Galatians, Paul states, "There can be neither Jew nor Greek; there can be neither bond nor free; there can be no male and female; for ye are all one man in Christ Jesus" (Gal. 3:28, ASV). In our day this great apostolic truth is beginning to have fresh meaning and blessing. We live in the

age of emancipated womanhood. The same Gospel that over
the years has been instrumental in the release of many victims from the bondage of slavery has also liberated woman
and restored her to her rightful place beside man.

It took centuries for the Christian Church to realize that
slavery was incompatible with the teachings of Christ,
and longer still for her to realize that God has sometimes
given a woman a great message for her age and the
world. . . . And if in our age God has given women who
both can evangelize the world and teach the Church, it
is not for the Church to reject this gift of the ascended
Christ, but to use it with thankfulness and wisdom
inspired by His Spirit.[2]

It is our conviction that God the Holy Spirit does at times
use women in a public ministry; and since the Holy Spirit is
the author of Scripture, such ministry must be in full accord
with inspired Scripture. Truly, the liberating Gospel of our
Lord Jesus Christ has freed women to exercise their spiritual
gifts in a public as well as in a private sphere.
    Mr. E.R. Pitman comments:

It is only in Christian lands that women occupy their
proper place. In all other countries they are drudges,
slaves, or victims; but equals or companions, *never!*
Christianity in a large measure revokes the curse which
the Fall [presumably] imposed on women, and Christ
made the sexes more equal by coming as a man, and
being born of a woman. He not only raised the standard
of our common humanity by wearing our human nature,
but he took the bitterness out of the woman's lot by
honoring and adopting motherhood. From that time all
motherhood became brighter and holier, and all womanhood grander yet tenderer.[3]

We believe the contention by certain church leaders that

a woman shall have no public voice violates the balanced teaching of the Bible. Their opinion is based mainly on the Apostle Paul's words in 1 Corinthians 14:34-35 and 1 Timothy 2:12, where they insist that Paul imposes imperative silence upon women and permits them to raise their voices only in women's meetings. Any such teaching springs almost entirely from these short passages of Scripture, which if properly understood, harmonize with the great mass of Scripture that sanctions a woman's public ministry.

Earlier in his letter to the Corinthians Paul permits women to pray and to prophesy in a local assembly if they be properly attired: "Every woman that prayeth or prophesieth with her head uncovered dishonoureth her head" (1 Cor. 11:5). In the Book of Acts we read of various mixed prayer meetings where women apparently participated in praying and prophesying. In 1 Timothy 2:8-9, Paul exhorts both men and women to the exercise of prayer. For prophesying, both sexes have "the threefold warrant of inspired prediction (Acts 2:17), of primitive practice (Acts 21:9), and of apostolic provision[4] (1 Cor. 11:5)."

In coming to our conclusions concerning woman's true liberty, we cannot ignore the lessons to be learned from the spiritual life of the church. On the pages of church history we find record of many women anointed for outstanding Christian ministry or leadership. Such anointing does not controvert the Scriptures but is and always will be in harmony with God's inerrant Word.

Chapter Two

LEARNING FROM HEBREW HISTORY

The status of the Israelite woman has always been far above her standing in the pagan world. As we trace back into patriarchal times, we find the highest regard for womanhood; decisions on the domestic level were jointly made by husband and wife.

The fifth commandment of the decalogue reads, "Honor thy father and thy mother: that thy days may be long upon the land which the Lord thy God giveth thee" (Ex. 20:12). The mother was equally honored with the father. In Leviticus 19:3 the mother is actually named first: "Ye shall fear every man his mother, and his father."

Then note the strong words of Agur in Proverbs 30:17: "The eye that mocketh at his father, and despiseth to obey his mother, the ravens of the valley shall pick it out, and the young eagle shall eat it."

When Solomon became king, he honored his mother to the extent of promising her whatsoever she might request: "Ask on, my mother: For I will not say thee nay" (1 Kings 2:20).

And we cannot pass over the words of King Lemuel "that his mother taught him" (Prov. 31:1). His godly mother was honored of God to be the author of a well-known chapter of the Scriptures: Proverbs 31—a detailed description of the ideal woman, the true woman. This vivid portrait of the "virtuous woman" was simply the outgrowth of the wholesome teaching in the Mosaic theological system.

In Israel's family life the lot of the woman was immeasurably above her position in the contemporary heathen nations of that world. Daughters and sisters were honored and given special protection in Israel. A son might be sold, but not a daughter; she could not be bargained over as a bond servant (Ex. 21:7-11). For example, Jacob's sons championed the cause of Hebrew women's rights when they took vengeance on the men of Shechem for having abused their sister Dinah (Genesis 34).

Sarah

In the case of Abraham and Sarah we have the first account in Scripture of the calling and training of a family that was to bring blessing to all the human race. Let us, then, note briefly the interrelations of these two.

During his early walk of faith Abram made two serious missteps. The first was through a lack of *faith*, when during a threatened famine in Canaan he went down into Egypt. The second was through a lack of *courage*, when fearing for his own life, he persuaded his wife to utter a half truth; "Say, I pray thee, thou art my sister" (Gen. 12:13). Sarah was indeed Abram's half sister, but she was also his wife; and she was at fault in obeying him in this respect, sharing with him in an intentional lie.

The Apostle Peter appropriately points women to the example of Sarah who "obeyed Abraham, calling him lord" (1 Peter 3:6). Yet God commanded the old patriarch in one of the strongest passages in the Bible to obey his wife: "And God said unto Abraham, Let it not be grievous in thy sight because of the lad [Ishmael] and because of thy bondwoman; in all that Sarah hath said unto thee, hearken unto her voice [*listen to her*, NASB]; for in Isaac shall thy seed be called" (Gen. 21:12). The same Hebrew word translated "hearken unto" in this verse is correctly translated "obey" in Genesis 22:18 and in almost 90 other places in the Old Testament. So here Abraham was bidden to *obey* what Sarah told him to do.

In this family dispute between husband and wife, the husband was wrong; the wife was right. God revealed to Abraham that he must obey Sarah, for she was right and scriptural and in divine order. It is here evident that Sarah as Abraham's helper had God's direction as she instructed her husband. Abraham was the head of the household, but Sarah was his discerning partner, not his chattel or slave.

These occasions in this great patriarchal household clearly set forth the relation of obedience and respect of husband and wife as being mutual and reciprocal; and the striking instance is that of Abraham submitting to the righteous demand of Sarah, though normally she would have been in subjection to him.

Rebekah

Rebekah's wishes were respected when she was sought as a wife for Isaac. Abraham's servant was divinely led to the woman of God's choice, yet Rebekah had to make her own decision. Her parents would not decide for her but said to the servant, "We will call the damsel and enquire at her mouth." When Rebekah appeared they said unto her, "Wilt thou go with this man?" Without any hesitation, feeling that she was being led of God no less surely than was Abraham's servant, with the voice of firm decision she replied, "I will go" (Gen. 24:57-58). The fact of her personal freedom in this decision is very evident.

Rachel and Leah

The mutual and reciprocal relationship of husband and wife again finds illustration in the story of Jacob when he sought the counsel of his wives, Rachel and Leah. After twenty years in Padan-Aram he heard God's call to return to the land of his fathers. "And Jacob went and called Rachel and Leah to the field" and consulted with them. Their reply reflects their agreement with Jacob's proposal: "Whatsoever God has said unto thee, do" (Genesis 31:3-4, 14-16). These women were not mere servants of a manipulating Jacob, but rather important decisions were jointly made in this household.

Abigail

Consider also the case of Abigail, that noble woman who risked the wrath of her husband by promptly sending a large peace offering to appease the anger of David. Without her husband's knowledge or consent, she took matters in her own hands and successfully entreated David for the life of her foolish and worthless husband, knowing full well how he had foolishly refused to give David anything for his men (1 Sam. 25:1-35).

The above examples furnish ample evidence of the high status accorded Hebrew women in early Bible times. As someone has aptly said, "There never was a time from Sarah to Mary when woman was not held in honor."

Throughout Old Testament history women's right to speak in the name of the Lord was never questioned. More than that, women were admitted now and then to highest positions of teaching and leadership and government.

Miriam

Born in an Israelite home during the bondage in Egypt, Miriam was the older sister of Aaron and Moses. Doubtless she was the maid who watched over the ark of bulrushes in which the infant Moses was laid. Later Miriam was associated with Moses and Aaron in God's deliverance of the Children of Israel from Egypt. Through the Prophet Micah God reminds the nation Israel of this past deliverance: "I brought thee up out of the land of Egypt, and redeemed thee out of the house of bondage; and I sent before thee Moses, and Aaron, and Miriam" (Micah 6:4, ASV). So God chose not only her brothers but Miriam, a woman, as one who had part in Israel's deliverance from slavery. What an honor for a woman!

After this deliverance Miriam took part in the great song of Moses which celebrated God's triumph over Pharaoh at the Red Sea crossing. "And Miriam the prophetess, the sister of Aaron, took a timbrel in her hand; and all the women went out after her with timbrels and dances. And Miriam answered them, 'Sing ye to the Lord, for He hath triumphed gloriously; the horse and his rider hath he thrown into the sea' " (Ex. 15:20-21).

Noted historian Dr. Rawlinson takes these words of Miriam to be a sort of refrain which was sung at the close of each stanza in the song. He says, "In Miriam we have the first of that long series of religious women presented to us in Holy Scripture who are not merely pious and God-fearing, but exercise a quasi-ministerial office."[1]

We might observe that if absolute silence of women before men had been the rule at this time, that outburst of praise under Miriam at the Red Sea would have been improper. "Yet stolid of soul must be those whose heart does not throb with the ecstasy of that hour of Jehovah's triumph and feel that those dancing feet and clanging timbrels and ringing voices were a fitting accompaniment to that thrilling moment."[2]

Deborah

Deborah is another remarkable character, one who is considered among the wisest of all Old Testament women. She was indeed a famous and fearless patriot, chosen of God to liberate her distressed and defeated people.

Many and varied were the accomplishments of her brilliant career. She was "the wife of Lapidoth" (Jud. 4:4) and "a mother in Israel" (Jud. 5:7); she was one of a number of women in Scripture distinguished as a prophetess; and more than that, she was a competent judge and warrior-leader. But apparently this public activity did not render her "in any way neglectful of her conjugal and wifely duties."[3]

As a prophetess Deborah discerned the mind of God for her times and declared the purpose of God to her people. Stately in person "she dwelt under the palm tree . . . between Ramah and Bethel in Mount Ephraim: and the Children of Israel came up to her for judgment" (Jud. 4:5). Does someone contend that Deborah's judgeship was merely that of a referee settling some local disputes? Is this all that is meant by Deborah's having judged Israel for forty years? Did she not dispense righteousness and justice and mercy; and after her victory over the nation's foes, did she not rule with justice a land that "had rest [from war for] forty years"? (Jud. 5:31)

Early in her judgeship Deborah was greatly exercised about Israel's oppression under Jabin, King of Hazor. Evidently God had told Barak to take the necessary steps to deliver Israel, but he lacked the courage or the know-how or the seasonable time to launch the conquest. When this was made known to Deborah, she sent for Barak and said to him, "Hath not the Lord God of Israel commanded, saying, 'Go and draw toward Mount Tabor, and take with thee ten thousand men . . . ? And I will draw unto thee to the river Kishon Sisera, the captain of Jabin's army, with his chariots and his multitude; and I will deliver him into thine hand' " (Jud. 4:6-7).

Barak was fearful, however, and said unto her, "If thou wilt go with me, then I will go: but if thou wilt not go with me, then I will not go" (Jud. 4:8). Barak's obvious dependence upon Deborah indicates the great degree of leadership which she had attained in Israel at this time. The whole initiative of the campaign lay in the hands of this female warrior-leader, judge, and companion in battle.

Her reply to Barak was simply, "I will surely go with thee: notwithstanding the journey that thou takest shall not be for thine honour; for the Lord shall sell Sisera into the hand of a woman. And Deborah arose, and went with Barak to Kedesh" (Jud. 4:9). So just as she had prophesied, the glory of the victory did go into "the hand of a woman," even the hand of Jael, the Kenite (Jud. 4:15-21).

After thoroughly routing the mighty Jabin and his hosts, Deborah and Barak sang the magnificent eulogy of praise to God that we read in Judges 5:2-31. Obviously Deborah the prophetess was the authoress and leader in this song (Jud. 5:3, 7, 9). Barak joined in antiphonal response while it was being sung, just as Miriam and her women did in the song of Moses.

Was Deborah indeed a woman whom God in His sovereignty chose to be the spiritual leader and judge when there was apparently no man found suitable for the occasion? The Scriptures plainly show that as judge she exercised authority in matters of legal dispute; as prophetess she proclaimed God's Word to the people; and under divine inspiration she composed one of the "grandest outbursts of impassioned poetry in the Bible."[4]

At the time of the judges it seems that men of faith and heroism had largely disappeared from Israel, that Joshuas and Calebs were no more, and the people were crushed in spirit. But "man's extremity is God's opportunity." To our thinking the individuals God singled out seem in several respects most unqualified to occupy the positions to which God called them, yet the divine power and wisdom were justified in Israel's victory through Deborah's skillful leadership and Jael's deed. "God hath chosen the foolish things of the world to confound the wise; and God hath chosen the weak things of the world to confound the things which are mighty; . . . that no flesh should glory in His presence" (1 Cor. 1:27, 29).

Hannah
So well known is the story of Hannah that we need dwell only

on traits of character relevant to this study. Her husband Elkanah had two wives, Hannah and Peninnah. The latter had children while Hannah had none, for the Lord "had shut up her womb" (1 Sam. 1:5). Of course God foreknew what He was going to do through her great son Samuel; hence His action in shutting up Hannah's womb was a remarkable providence for heaven's greater glory, even though it was for a time a cause of deep distress for this "woman of a sorrowful spirit" (1 Sam. 1:15). She was indeed a lily in a thorny domestic situation. Hers was a polygamous house, with heartless Peninnah having children, all the while torturing and tantalizing Hannah for being barren; but though "childless, Hannah was not prayerless. [Though] barren she still believed."[5]

Hannah's whispered prayer of agony was misinterpreted by Eli, the high priest, who accused her of being drunk. Incidentally Hannah must not have been veiled to any extent, for Eli saw that her lips moved in prayer. After she had explained her deep desire for a son, Eli responded prophetically: "Go in peace; and the God of Israel grant thee thy petition" (1 Sam. 1:17). In due time Samuel was born. After Hannah had weaned the child, she presented him in the house of the Lord, saying, "Oh my lord, as thy soul liveth, my lord, I am the woman that stood by thee here, praying unto the Lord. For this child I prayed; and the Lord hath given me my petition which I asked of Him: therefore also have I lent him to the Lord; as long as he liveth he shall be lent to the Lord" (1 Sam. 1:26-28).

Then Hannah in the spirit of prayer and prophecy burst forth in such praise that her song became the basis of the Magnificat—the Virgin Mary's psalm of praise eleven centuries later (see Luke 1:46-55). As Hannah's inspired prayer poured forth in his presence, Eli neither interrupted nor reproved her; and Hannah was uninhibited by the law of public "silence," later imposed by some New Testament theologians. Simply out of the abundance of the heart, her mouth spoke:

My heart rejoiceth in the Lord, mine horn is exalted in
the Lord: my mouth is enlarged over mine enemies;
because I rejoice in Thy salvation. There is none holy as
the Lord: for there is none beside Thee: neither is there
any rock like our God. Talk no more so exceeding
proudly; let not arrogancy come out of your mouth: for
the Lord is a God of knowledge, and by Him actions are
weighed. (1 Sam. 2:1-3)

The rest of her hymn of thanksgiving sounds like a Davidic
psalm of victory. So Eli, having heard Hannah's inspired
paean of public praise in the house of the Lord, did not
silence her but rather recorded her song for the benefit of
unborn generations.

Huldah

In Huldah we have another instance of God's choosing a
woman to be His prophetic voice. She became God's mouthpiece to the kingdom of Judah in a day of grievous departure
from the Lord. During her time of ministry, young king
Josiah came to the throne and began to do "that which was
right in the sight of the Lord" (2 Kings 22:2). He set about to
purge Judah and Jerusalem of the pagan worship which his
predecessors had promoted. To accomplish this, his first
move was to restore the temple, which had fallen into a sad
state of disrepair and filth. At that time the long lost "book of
the law" was discovered in the midst of the rubbish; then
Shaphan, the scribe, brought the book to the king and read
from it. At once the pious young king rent his clothes,
realizing afresh Judah's serious state of decline and the immi-
nence of God's wrath to be poured out upon them because of
their disobedience. The situation was so threatening that
Josiah took counsel with Hilkiah the priest and other principal men to know what should be done.

Significant at this point is the fact that Hilkiah did not
consult with Jeremiah, the prophet of Anathoth, nor with

other contemporary prophets, such as Habakkuk and Zephaniah, but he with four other men "went unto Huldah the prophetess . . . and they communed with her" (2 Kings 22:14). Apparently they realized that "the spirit of prophecy, that inestimable treasure, was sometimes put not only into *earthen* vessels, but into the *weaker* vessels, *that the excellency of the power might be of God.*"[6] Perhaps the leading men in Israel recalled how Miriam had helped to lead Israel out of Egypt and how Deborah had once successfully judged Israel for forty years. Now they recognized Huldah, the prophetess, as one having the mind of God to instruct them. These emissaries of the king had greater assurance of Huldah's prophetic commission than of any other true prophets in the land. No doubt they had consulted her on other occasions and found that the wisdom in her mouth was truth to be relied upon, and they knew how to value that wisdom.

Huldah sent back word to Josiah: "Thus saith the Lord God of Israel, Tell the man that sent you to me . . ." And three more times in five verses this prophetess authoritatively said, "thus saith the Lord" (2 Kings 22:15-19). Huldah was God's mouthpiece, speaking His will to the king. She spoke the truth, she warned the people, and she comforted King Josiah.

Here we see that God in His sovereignty chose a woman, even when men prophets were available, to interpret the warnings of Scripture for King Josiah, who had sent to inquire of her. Likewise God has chosen other women on occasion to exercise public testimony of praise, to exercise the gift of prophecy as the mouthpiece of God, and at times even to exercise authority over men. Such instances of audible expression and important public participation in the Jewish community give women a permanent place in Old Testament religious history.

Esther

Queen Esther—what a historical character was she, thrust as a young woman into a position of public prominence and power in the Persian Empire! As a supreme heroine, she came to the kingdom just in time to save her people from national disaster. In the hour of her severest testing we hear her agonizing cry: "How can I endure to see the evil that shall come unto my people? or how can I endure to see the destruction of my kindred?" (Es. 8:6) In her greatest hour of crisis, Esther dared to risk her life for her people, saying, "If I perish, I perish" (Es. 4:16). Thus by her heroic patriotism she won for her nation a great deliverance.

At a crucial time in their history it pleased God to use Esther as an instrument to save His people from their enemies. As a result, this Persian queen was crowned with glory and honor and has been remembered by the Jews ever since at the annual feast of Purim.

Is a virtuous woman "a crown to her husband"? (Prov. 12:4) Yes, indeed, and Esther was truly a crown of glory to King Ahasuerus. She honored the king as her "head." In turn God used this humble yet strong-minded woman as an instrument of His providence for the working out of His glorious purpose for His people.

Queen Esther along with Mordecai was so exalted under King Ahasuerus that they wrote official letters to the 127 provinces "with all authority" (Es. 9:29-30). Does the natural mind puzzle over the problem of how a woman who should not be domineering could at the same time be providentially placed in the position of authority? Was not Queen Esther in authority because she was so completely under the higher authority of Ahasuerus? And "since the word of the king is authoritative" (Ecc. 8:4, NASB), no less was the word of Queen Esther regarded "with all authority."

Esther was one of heaven's "weaker vessels" who must have had a word from God similar to that which came to the Apostle Paul: "He hath said unto me, My grace is sufficient for thee: for My power is made perfect in weakness" (2 Cor. 12:9, ASV). Her response must have been, "When I am weak, then am I strong" (2 Cor. 12:10). Let every "weaker vessel" when called of God rejoice that "God hath chosen the weak things of the world to confound the things which are mighty" (1 Cor. 1:27).

A Great Host

The outstanding women mentioned above were not the only instances of the prophetic gift being bestowed on and exercised by women of the Old Testament. The following passage indicates that there were many other female voices: "The Lord gives the command. The women who proclaim the good tidings are a great host" (Ps. 68:11, NASB). In his commentary Dr. Adam Clarke gives this literal translation of Psalm 68:11: "Of the female preachers there was a great host." He adds,

> Some think [this] refers to the *women*, who, with music, songs, and dances, celebrated the victories of the Israelites over their enemies. But the publication of *good news*, or of any *joyful event*, belongs to the *women*. It was they who announced it to the people at large; and to this universal custom, which prevails to the *present day*, the Psalmist alludes.[7]

Dr. Clarke's literal translation of Isaiah 40:9 is also illuminating: "O daughter that bringest good tidings to Zion, get thee up into the high mountain; O thou [woman], that publisheth good tidings to Jerusalem, lift up thy voice with strength; lift it up, be not afraid; say unto the cities of Judah, Behold your God!" He further comments,

> The office of announcing and celebrating such glad tidings as are here spoken of, belonged peculiarly to the women. On occasion of any great public success, a signal victory, or any other joyful event, it was usual for the women to gather together, and with music, dances, and song, to publish and celebrate the happy news. Thus,

after the passage of the Red Sea, Miriam, and all the women, with timbrels in their hands, formed a chorus, and joined the men in their triumphant song, dancing, and throwing in alternately the refrain or burden of the song. . . .

So in this place, Jehovah having given the word by His prophet, the joyful tidings of the restoration of Zion, and of God's returning to Jerusalem, . . . the women are exhorted by the prophet, to publish the joyful news with a loud voice.[8]

In all of the Old Testament there is not one sentence forbidding woman to speak publicly. If the Lord Himself on occasion employed an Esther or a Deborah, may we not expect Him in sovereign wisdom to do the same today? A certain liberty-loving Plymouth brother makes this observation:

Those who study history in the light of the Old Testament will have no difficulty in seeing the hand of God in putting the great Victoria upon the throne and in keeping her there so long. I myself knew an elderly sister in Christ, one of God's princesses, who actually, though not nominally or obstrusively, was "bishop" over two or three country assemblies, guiding them with a heavenly wisdom that no brother then in that district possessed. And I have seen the same thing in foreign lands.[9]

Chapter Three

WOMEN AT CREATION AND AFTER THE FALL

What does God's Word in the Old Testament teach regarding the status of women? God made this divine pronouncement in Genesis 1:26-27:

> Let Us make man in Our image, after Our likeness: and let them have dominion over the fish of the sea, and over the fowl of the air, and over the cattle, and over all the earth, and over every creeping thing that creepeth upon the earth. So God created man in His own image, in the image of God created He him; male and female created He them.

The statements "let Us make man," "let them have dominion," and "God created man in His own image . . . male and female created He them" make it clear that the word *man* is used in the generic or universal sense as including both the man and the woman. So man was created "male and female" and joint dominion was committed to them. "Let them have dominion" shows that woman was recognized as equal with man. Joint dominion was given to Eve along with Adam over the earth and all creatures.

A Help Meet

Note also God's testimony to man's needs: "It is not good
that the man should be alone; I will make him an help meet
for him" (Gen. 2:18). This must mean that the man "constituted but one half of the human race. . . . The Divine purpose could only be realized in God furnishing the other
half."[1]   "This is a proper place to correct a current and
erroneous conception of the narrative in Genesis," writes Dr.
A.T. Pierson. He continues:

> God saw that man could not reach an *ideal state* in
> solitude. Quite apart from the *peopling* of the earth, there
> was the question of man's own need and welfare. "And
> God said, I will make him an help, meet for him."
> Observe this is not a compound word—help-meet.
> This may seem a small matter, but in part, upon a
> mistaken and mischievous conception of this text, has
> been built up a system of domestic tyranny and injustice
> that [has] lasted for ages, on one hand developing in the
> man marital despotism, and on the other, wifely subjec-
> tion and servitude, and the degradation of woman.
> What God *did* say was literally, *"one, over against
> him,"* that is his *counterpart*, correspondent, his other
> half. No superiority on his part, nor inferiority on her
> part, is necessarily implied. There is indeed a marital
> headship, entrusted to the husband and emphasized in
> the New Testament as well as the Old; but it is a
> headship not to be held in wilfulness or selfishness, nor
> exercised in arbitrary authority but in unselfish devo-
> tion, provision and protection, leadership and love.[2]

So we see that "help meet" involves two separate words.
Meet modifies *help* and means "fit" or "ideally suited." God
would provide a counterpart for the man—his other self. She

is "a helping being, in which, as soon as he sees [her] he may recognize himself."[3]

This equality of the sexes is made plain in the formation of Eve. In Genesis 2:22 we read, "The Lord God made [*builded He into*, Hebrew] a woman from the rib He had taken out of the man, and He brought her to the man" (NIV). Matthew Henry expresses this equality very beautifully when he says,

> The woman was made *of a rib out of the side of Adam;* not made out of his head to rule over him, nor out of his feet to be trampled upon by him, but out of his side to be equal with him, under his arm to be protected, and near his heart to be beloved.[4]

Woman was thus of the same nature as man, of the same flesh and blood, and of the same constitution in all respects. Consequently as woman she had equal powers, faculties, and rights. The very nature of her creation was meant to ensure man's affection and stimulate his esteem.

Eve was indeed no mere helpmate. Rather in her person and constitution she was suitable to be his companion both socially and intellectually; "Eve was not an appendage to Adam but his complement."[5] As Adam's complement Eve would find her freedom and joy in glad submission to the divine order—a submission as far from servility as heaven is from hell.

Bruce Milne in his book *Know the Truth* sees in Genesis 2:18 woman's full equality with man:

> "A helper fit for him" . . . has the force of "equal and adequate to." . . . There is no hint of inferiority; woman is not man's slave or subordinate, but stands in her integrity by his side before God. Her intrinsic dignity is seen at its clearest in Scripture in the gospels. Jesus instinctively conferred equality on the women He met and ministered to.[6]

Dr. A.T. Pierson further clarifies the issue:

The practical inference, too often gathered from the record in Genesis, is that man was created as woman's lord and master—his imperial majesty, the man, to be Lord of Creation; and woman—God's last and best creative product, to be, if not his lackey, at best his servant, to bow at his feet, wait on him, do his bidding, without any way or will of her own, to sink alike her individuality and independence in his pleasure and caprice. And, under the sanction of this perverted notion, woman has been degraded for centuries and milleniums into a slave of man's despotism, a victim of his tyranny, and even a tool of his passions, when God meant her to be his companion and equal, his helper and counsellor. The historic outcome of such perversion has been a long history of social wrong—polygamy with its harem and seraglio; domestic and social seclusion and exclusion, with its zenana; capricious divorce with its companion and consequence—adulterous unions, and a whole brood of kindred curses and crimes.[7]

A Shared Responsibility

To man—male and female—was given a definite mission and commission: a charge "to multiply" and "replenish" the earth and to "have dominion" over it. The two are one and equal in nature, in life, and in commission, the woman having a vital part and responsibility with man in the purpose of God for the promotion and the propagation of the race. The woman is not man's slave, but the interests of both are one and mutual, and they are by love to serve one another. It has been the failure of both sexes to understand and fulfill their individual roles that has led to many of their miseries. Unfortunately some of God's Christian leaders have unwittingly contributed to this tragedy.

Henry Ward Ayer once made this wise observation:

One of the great proofs of creation is the *complement of sexes*. Nothing but Personality and Plan could bring this to pass. I speak not only of the physical complement, but the mental and the spiritual. How could chance ever produce the strong characteristics of the male and then to balance these characteristics produce the tenderness and sympathy and fine moral fibre of the female. . . .

The fact of the matter is that neither is complete without the other.[8]

Dr. Pierson shows how both man and woman are needed:

Man is no doubt in some respects superior to woman, in capacity for leadership, active and aggressive enterprise; and he has proved historically to surpass her in inventive genius and public achievement. But he is also inferior in heart qualities, in moral intuition, in affectional depth, in emotional sensibility, in capacity for suffering and sacrifice. Each has proficiencies and deficiencies. What one has, the other lacks, and conversely. Comparisons are often individuous because unfair. When things are not *alike* each must be looked at apart from the other; and so man and woman must be studied, in order to understand how each is, in a higher sense a part of the other, or rather a part of the perfect whole.[9]

Regarding marriage he presents the divine ideal:

God's original ideal then must be kept before us: One man and one woman, mutually in sympathy, intellectually, morally, and religiously, united in a partnership whose association is more intimate and tender, perfect and permanent than any other, displacing even filial and fraternal ties, so that a man shall leave father and mother and cleave unto his wife, they being no more twain, but one flesh, losing almost individuality and duality in a higher sacred mutuality and unity.[10]

Male and female oneness has been clearly set forth in the creation account in Genesis. Therefore any demeaning of woman—enslaving her, subjugating her, or treating her as inferior—goes contrary to God's original plan and purpose. Man and woman were created equal in all essential respects—in person, in nature, in dignity, and in commission. They are one in Christ Jesus.

Did God Curse Woman in Genesis 3:16?

In the account of the Fall of man (Gen. 3) we find that Satan so beguiled Eve by his "craftiness" (2 Cor. 11:3, ASV) that she was "thoroughly deceived" (Greek) and "fell into trans-gression" (1 Tim. 2:14, NASB). Then she gave of the fruit to Adam, and he ate it. Eve was deceived, but Adam sinned with his eyes wide open, for, as Paul tell us, he was not deceived; he chose deliberately. She was a victimized sinner; he was a deliberate sinner. His guilt in the Fall, therefore, was greater than that of Eve. Although Eve was first to take of the forbidden fruit, Adam was more guilty because he was not deceived as Eve was. God's Word is explicit: "Through one man sin entered into the world, and death through sin" (Rom. 5:12, NASB). Scripture does not lay the blame for the entrance of sin into the world on Eve but rather on Adam: "in Adam all die" (1 Cor. 15:22).

Now let us consider God's Word to Satan, to Adam, and especially His Word to Eve—"the law" to which many expos-itors believe Paul refers in 1 Corinthians 14:34: "Let your women keep silence in the churches . . . as also saith the law."

When God appeared to the fallen pair in the garden, they "hid themselves from the presence of the Lord God amongst the trees of the garden" (Gen. 3:8). God questioned Adam, "Where art thou? . . . Hast thou eaten of the tree, whereof I commanded thee that thou shouldst not eat?" (Gen. 3:9, 11) Note that this challenge of God was to Adam, not to Eve. In reply Adam said, "The woman whom Thou gavest to be with me, she gave me of the tree, and I did eat" (Gen. 3:12). Adam sought to excuse himself by laying the blame on Eve and more than that on God Himself.

God then turned to Eve and asked, "What is this that thou hast done?" Eve replied, "The serpent beguiled me, and I did eat" (Gen. 3:13). This was a true statement of fact in which Eve made no excuse but admitted that she had been deceived by Satan's subtlety. She did not seek to put any blame on God as Adam did.

Turning first to the serpent, God begins to pronounce judgment (Gen. 3:14-15). Having first put a curse on the serpent, God said, "I will put (*am putting*, lit.) enmity between you and the woman, and between your seed and her seed." Here is a most remarkable statement. Eve had already aroused the enmity of Satan by exposing him as a deceiver. God is now widening this enmity; indeed He will widen the enmity between Satan's seed (those in the future who will take Satan's side against God), and Eve's seed (those who will side with God against Satan)—a seed which would ultimately be headed up in Christ.

Then with Christ directly in view, God said to Satan: "He shall bruise you on the head, and you shall bruise Him on the heel." This statement is the first intimation in the Bible of the good news that the "seed" of the woman, Christ, will bruise Satan's "head" in a final and decisive defeat and overthrow, though Satan will be permitted to bruise Christ's "heel." (Both of these bruisings took place at the cross.)

Judgment on Eve

Turning next to Eve, God pronounced judgment: "I will greatly multiply thy sorrow and thy conception [sighing, LXX]; in sorrow thou shalt bring forth children; and thy desire shall be to thy husband, and he shall rule over thee" (Gen. 3:16). This pronouncement calls for very careful consideration, especially the concluding clause. Dr. Katherine Bushnell and others point out that these words as translated in our English versions have been misunderstood.

In the first place, the Hebrew word *teshuqa* has been wrongly translated *desire* in our English versions. Lewis in Lange's commentary declares: "The sense of this word is not *libido*, or sensual desire."[11] It is apparently derived from a verb meaning "to run" or "to run back and forth," which would require frequent "turning." *Teshuqa* occurs only three times in the Old Testament—here in this clause, next in Genesis 4:7, and lastly in the Song of Songs 7:10. In all three verses the *Septuagint* renders it by the Greek equivalent to our word *turning,* and so does the Syrian Peshitto version, the Ethiopian, the old Latin version, and several other versions. In fact, of twelve ancient versions all but two translate *teshuqa* with the word "turning" in one or in all three of these verses.[12] We believe the verse should read: "Thou art turning away to thy husband, and he will rule over thee." Eve is "turning" from God, and He warns her that if she does that, she will fall under the dominion of Adam.

Professor H.B. Mitchell of Boston University, in his book, *The World Before Abraham*, has well represented the general sense of the phrase translated, "thy desire shall be to thy husband." He says,

> It must mean mere inclination, or something equally removed from sensuality: and in [Song 7:10] . . . it has the force of affection, devotion. ["His turning is towards me."] There is therefore ground for the opinion that the author in this passage [Gen. 3:16] intended to make Jehovah say that the very tenderness of the woman for the husband would enable him to make and keep her his inferior.[13]

It seems clear that the sense of "desire," often interpreted as "lust," has come to us in the "Ten Curses of Eve" out of the Talmud (a compilation of the traditions of the Jews.)[14]

In the second place the use of the word *shall* in "shall rule over thee" is unfortunate. Professor Moulton (a Greek schol-

ar) has observed, "The use of 'shall' when prophecy is dealing with future time is often particularly unfortunate," as
suggesting an imperative, a decree, or a law. It is very
important and crucial in the understanding of Genesis 3:16
whether we view it as a *prophecy* or as a *penalty*. The use of
shall here no more denotes a decree than it does in God's
Word to Satan, "thou *shalt* bruise his heel," in which God in
no way commands Satan to do this. The statement, therefore,
of Genesis 3:16 in no way expresses a "law" of God for Eve
and for future woman's subjection to man; it is rather a
warning, a *prophecy*, a *prediction* to Eve that as her "turning"
was to her husband rather than to God, her husband *would*
"rule over her." The latter part of God's Word here is
"descriptive rather than prescriptive"[15] that man would lord it
over her.

The Misunderstanding Perpetuated

This misunderstanding of God's Word to Eve has a bearing
on the interpretation of Paul's "as also saith the law" (1 Cor.
14:34). As already noted, many expositors see in this *law* a
reference to God's Word to Eve in Genesis 3:16, although
such a law is not found in the Mosaic Law but only in the
Jewish oral law.

When the Jewish remnant returned to the Holy Land
from exile, their religious leaders proceeded to frame their
"authoritative" interpretations of the Old Testament, which
became a kind of second law for the nation. These interpretations were the traditions of the elders with which Christ so
often came into conflict because they made "the Word of
God of none effect through [their] tradition" (Mark 7:13).
Later these traditions were put in writing in the *Talmud*. In
this hitherto *oral* law the Jewish teachers maintained that in
Genesis 3:16 God had pronounced "ten curses" against Eve
and indirectly on women in general.

Some of these "oral laws," later embodied in the *Talmud*,
are as follows:

Rather have the roll of the law burned than have it
taught to a woman. (Rabbi Eleazer)
It is shame for a woman to let her voice be heard among
men. (Megilla)
The testimony of one hundred women is not equal to
that of one man.
The voice of a woman is filthy nakedness. (Taanith)

The *Talmud* described a woman "sinner" as "she who
transgresseth the Law of Moses and the Jewish Law.
. . . 'The Jewish law, that is, what the daughters of Israel
follow though it be not written.' " A pertinent item in the
Jewish oral law states, "If she appear abroad with her head
uncovered, if she spin in the streets,"[16] that would be a
transgression of the law. In fact the *Talmud* prescribes that if a
woman goes about in public with her head uncovered, she
should be considered unchaste and can therefore be divorced
by her husband. Among the Jews,

It was the custom in the case of a woman accused of
adultery to have her hair "shorn or shaven," . . . at the
same time using the formula: "Because thou hast de-
parted from the manner of the daughters of Israel, who
go about with their head covered: . . . therefore that has
befallen thee which thou hast chosen."[17]

In view of these biased Jewish traditions it is not surprising that the Jewish male was taught to repeat regularly,
"Blessed be God that hath not made me a woman." Nor is it
surprising that even Christ's disciples marvelled that He
"talked with the woman" (John 4:27).
These Jewish oral laws, based upon a misunderstanding
or mistranslation of Genesis 3:16, not only have had an
important bearing upon the interpretation of the Apostle
Paul's words in 1 Corinthians 14:34 but also have colored the
views of some of the early church fathers. Tertullian (A.D.
160–230) for example had this to say concerning women:

And do you not know that you are (each) an
Eve? . . . *You* are the devil's gateway; *you* are the
unsealer of that (forbidden) tree; *you* are the first desert-
er of the divine law. *You* are she who persuaded him
[Adam] whom the devil himself was not valiant enough
to attack. *You* destroyed so easily God's image, man. On
account of *your* desert . . . even the very Son of God
had to die.[18]

Regarding the distortion of the Genesis passage, Mrs.
Penn-Lewis wrote,

We need not trouble about the rendering of Genesis
3:16, did we not find a reference to it placed again and
again in the margins of the N.T. [New Testament],
showing that the fundamental mistranslation in Genesis
perpetually coloured the minds of translators in inter-
preting the language of St. Paul. For instance, we find
in one version of the N.T. a note in the margin of 1 Cor.
11:3, saying, "cf. Genesis 3:16. *The woman's veil, or head
covering, is a symbol of this subordination*"; again in 1 Cor.
14:34, a marginal reference says, "cf. Genesis 3:16";
and yet again in 1 Timothy 2:11, to the word "subjection" is placed the reference, "cf. Genesis 3:16." All
showing that "Genesis 3:16" is supposed to interpret
the words of Paul in these particular passages in the
N.T.[19]

The Bible maintains the balanced responsibility of both
men and women in the Fall. Both are now fallen—equally
fallen—a depraved pair indeed.

Chapter Four

MALE AND FEMALE DISTINCTIVES

M en and women are indeed of equal dignity and mentality, each the complement of the other. Yet there are differences so distinct that "a masculine woman and a feminine man are monstrosities to be abhorred."[1] Therefore if we follow the scriptural pattern for women we must of necessity reject the radical feminism of the women's movement. In its attempt to correct the social injustice of the downgrading of women, this movement would dissolve the male and female distinctives, which are ordained by God.

We need not wonder what gave rise to this modern surge of social sentiment.

[It] arose because women in our society have not always been treated equally and with dignity. . . . Women entering the labor market haven't had the same opportunities for jobs and advancement that men have.

During the last twenty years, however, great strides have been made. Legislation has provided women the opportunity for equal pay for equal work, equal job opportunities, equal educational opportunities, equal credit opportunities, and many other rights they previously were denied.

And now the culmination of these legislative efforts: the ERA.[2]

We have not the least sympathy with the aims and goals of the ERA, which according to the literature of the radical feminists, are to "do away with family, love, marriage, heterosex, and religion."[3] Certainly no Bible-taught believer can endorse or have sympathy with the ERA. This is idolatry's modern Moloch that sings and dances about such slogans as equality, human rights, social justice, and so forth. Of course, we as Christians are liberated to be holy, to do right, to love mercy; liberated to be just what each was meant to be: men to be men and women to be women. Elisabeth Elliot reflects this liberty in the title of her book, *Let Me Be a Woman*.

The chief error of the ERA is the failure to recognize that while men and women are alike so that each is a part of the other, men are not exactly like women nor are women exactly like men. Since they are not alike, each must be considered apart from the other. Differences are to be recognized, not ignored or obliterated. Further, differences are to be cultivated— the man to become manly, and the woman to become womanly.

"Adam was first formed, then Eve" (1 Tim. 2:13), but by contrast Eve was the first to be entangled in transgression. "It was not Adam who was deceived, but the woman being quite deceived [*thoroughly deceived*, lit.], fell into transgression" (1 Tim. 2:14, NASB). The completeness of Eve's deception is set forth in 2 Corinthians 11:3, where it appears that the serpent thoroughly blinded and corrupted the mind of Eve by his craftiness. Evidently that old serpent, the devil, knew that the woman was more susceptible to guile and persuasion; therefore he tempted her in the absence of her husband. Denney states it this way: "The serpent beguiled Eve by his craftiness: he took advantage of her unsuspecting innocence to wile her away from her simple belief in God and obedience to Him."[4] Eve "was thoroughly deceived, and became involved in transgression" (1 Tim. 2:14, WEY). She yielded to the temptations of sense and the deceits of Satan.

> [It would seem that] this greater susceptibility to deception is revealed as a fact . . . inherent in the original constitution of the woman as compared with man. . . . It is, therefore, no fault or discredit to woman and it is compensated by a wealth of emotion, above that of the man, fitting her admirably to be the help answering to, that is complementing him.[5]

"Adam was not deceived" (1 Tim. 2:14); his fall was deliberate and not by deception. Adam definitely chose to go along with his wife instead of remaining loyal to the Lord God. Some would have us believe that the term *weaker vessel* in 1 Peter 3:7 implies that woman is an inferior character, but should we consider that Eve was inferior because first deceived? If so, when Adam succumbed to Eve's entreaty (she being regarded as the inferior of the two), where does that place Adam? Did not Adam show the greater and more deliberate wickedness in being misled by his wife, a mere mortal?

In forming Adam first before Eve, God designed man for headship and responsibility. Priority in creation sets forth priority in position. In 1 Timothy 2:12-13 Paul warns against a wife's failure to be under authority and argues for Adam's headship. Adam Clarke wisely comments, "God fitted man by the robust construction of his body to live a *public life*, to contend with difficulties, and to be capable of great exertions."[6]

Dr. Clarke further comments concerning the female as "being more delicately, and consequently more slenderly constructed."[7] In 1 Peter 3:7 she is called "the weaker vessel," that is, more frail and delicate by contrast with man's roughness and virility.

[Peter states that men are to give] "honour unto the wife

as unto the weaker vessel," using [their] superior strength and experience on her behalf, and thus *honouring* her by becoming her protector and support . . . . *Honour* signifies *maintenance* as well as *respect.*[8]

When Peter tells husbands to honor their wives, he voices a sentiment quite foreign to his world. It is well to remember that "to the Jewish rabbis, and in most oriental societies, honor and respect went one way only—up—while those beneath one socially were regarded with disdain."[9]

J.P. Lange quotes Martin Luther as follows: "Woman is weaker in body, more timid and less courageous than man, hence your treatment of her should be accordingly."[10] Lange himself states,

Woman is physically man's inferior, but it is doubtful whether she is so mentally. This is not in the writer's opinion a question of superiority or inferiority, but one of diversity. There are mental qualities in which woman excels man and others in which he excels her. They seem to be well balanced under equal advantages afforded to each. . . . Working together in one direction, [they] supply each other's defects and strengthen each other's powers. United this natural diversity blends in harmony.[11]

Husband and wife are both vessels—both weak but she the weaker. "As woman's weakness is relative, man also being a weak, frail vessel, he, mindful of his own weakness, ought the more readily to sympathize with the weaker."[12]

Woman's relative frailty by nature and her very feminine excellences tend to disqualify her from headship. Man, on the other hand, by his very constitution has qualities necessary for headship: "the equability of temper, practical shrewdness and discernment, the firm independent, regulative judgment, which are required to carry the leaders of important interests above first impressions and outside appearances."[13]

Dr. J.G. Morrison in his pamphlet, "Satan's Subtle Attack on Woman," sets forth the distinctives of men and women as follows:

[Man] is created for the battle, either with wild life, or wilder nature. . . . He loves to conquer. He is made for masterful supremacy! The woman's contribution to the race is charm, grace, affection, maternity, tenderness. She was never created to be a warrior. . . . She is not made to defend, but to be defended, inciting her champion to deeds of desperate valor, by her affection and enthusiasm. . . . She piles no stones for a cabin home [for that she was not created], but enters it, after it has been builded, and with the charm, touch, taste and intuition that only womanhood knows, makes the rude piles of stone, blossom into a home. . . . The union of the contribution of the man and the contribution of the woman, in holy harmony, makes the complete human, the ideal home, the divine environment, from which springs the new generation.[14]

Chapter Five

MINISTERING WOMEN IN THE GOSPELS

In the New Testament era women became increasingly prominent, participating in new ministries. According to Dr. A.T. Pierson,

> A marked feature of the New Acts of the Apostles is the apostolate of *woman*. From the day when Gabriel announced to that Virgin of Bethlehem her destiny as the human mother of the Son of God, woman has taken a new rank in history. Mary of Magdala, to whom first He appeared after His resurrection, was a forerunner of the thousands of her sex who should bear the good tidings of a risen Saviour. That outcast of Sychar who forgot her water-pot and hastened from the well to tell even the men of the city about the Messiah, forecast the myriad women who should forget themselves and all secular cares in the ministry to souls.[1]

Mary, the Mother of Jesus

Every godly Jewish mother entertained the hope that she might have the supreme honor of giving birth to the Messiah. Mary, mother of Jesus, realized this hope. Without dispute

this was the most incredible honor ever bestowed upon a
human being, even as the angel of God declares:

> And he came in unto her, and said, "Hail, thou that art
> highly favored, the Lord is with thee." . . . And the
> angel . . . said unto her, "The Holy Spirit shall come
> upon thee and the power of the Most High shall over-
> shadow thee: wherefore also the holy thing which is
> begotten shall be called the Son of God" [or as in the
> margin, "that which is to be born of thee shall be called
> holy, the Son of God"]. (Luke 1:28, 35, ASV)

Some time after this announcement Mary went to stay
with Elizabeth, the wife of the priest Zacharias. As soon as
Mary entered the home, Elizabeth, already six months with
child, was filled with the Holy Spirit,

> And she lifted up her voice with a loud cry and said,
> "Blessed art thou among women and blessed is the fruit
> of thy womb. And whence is this to me, that the mother
> of my Lord should come unto me? For behold, when the
> voice of thy salutation came into mine ears, the babe
> leaped in my womb for joy. And blessed is she that
> believeth; for there shall be a fulfillment of the things
> which have been spoken to her from the Lord." (Luke
> 1:41-45, ASV)

Mary responded in the immortal words of that wonderful
hymn of praise which we know as the Magnificat, a song
saturated with Old Testament prophecies and promises. We
cannot forbear quoting Mary to the full:

> My soul doth magnify the Lord, and my spirit hath
> rejoiced in God my Saviour. For He hath looked upon
> the low estate of His handmaid [*bondmaid*, Greek]: for
> behold, from henceforth all generations shall call me
> blessed. For He that is mighty hath done to me great

things; and holy is His name. And His mercy is unto generations and generations on them that fear Him. He hath showed strength with His arm; He hath scattered the proud in the imagination of their heart. He hath put down princes from their thrones, and hath exalted them of low degree. The hungry He hath filled with good things; and the rich He hath sent empty away. He hath given help to Israel His servant, that He might remember mercy (as He spake unto our fathers) toward Abraham and his seed forever. (Luke 1:46-55, ASV)

In this hymn we see Mary's prophetic gift as she shows how prophecy was being fulfilled, and reveals the glorious future for the nation Israel under the reign of Messiah.

Does someone wonder how Luke obtained these inspired words of Mary's hymn of praise? Did Mary herself remember the words and write them down? Or did Zacharias record the hymn after having heard it from the lips of Mary? We do not know, but in any case it must have been Mary alone who announced to the world and to all the ages the greatest single event of all history—the Incarnation.

It suffices us here to see that Elizabeth and Mary exercised the prophetic gift in the highest degree of public utterance. And we may be forever grateful that these witnesses, unable to be silent, opened their mouths in immortal praise and psalmody. "Mary belongs to those grand majestic females inspired with the spirit of prophecy, who [are] capable of influencing those who become rulers of men and also the destiny of nations."[2]

Anna

Now consider Anna, the first woman missionary to exercise the gift of prophecy in the New Testament. Mary and Joseph had brought the Baby Jesus into the temple, and the venerable Simeon, that "righteous and devout" man, had prophesied regarding the new-born Messiah. "Anna, a prophetess,

. . . coming up at that very hour . . . gave thanks unto God, and spake of Him [the Babe] to all of them that were looking for the redemption of Jerusalem" (Luke 2:36-38, ASV).

On this occasion we do not find Anna in some secluded little nook of the temple where the women were having a "sisters' meeting." Rather she, joining with the others, openly and audibly spoke to the congregation there assembled. Evidently she had been "doing it continually . . . [had] devoted herself to the ministry of an evangelist."[3] She was exercising her prophetic gift to the "edification and exhortation and consolation" (1 Cor. 14:3, ASV) of all the little flock who were anticipating the advent of the Messiah. "If this took place at the hour of prayer, it would account . . . for her having such an audience as the words imply."[4]

In those days Anna would not have so spoken in a synagogue, for the Jews never permitted a woman to speak in the synagogue. Manifestly there was more liberty in the temple. "Here we have without question a public testimony to a number of godly persons in the temple, both men and women, who shared Anna's aspirations."[5] Thus Anna, fulfilling her role as a prophetess, prayed and praised and proclaimed glad tidings of good things that had come to pass.

We surely believe that those whose hearts are filled with Christ, whether they be male or female, will not be silenced from speaking openly of Him to others but like Anna will witness audibly and continually. May her number grow exceedingly!

The Woman of Samaria

In his Gospel John tells the remarkable story of the woman of Samaria. In her we find a prejudiced woman, a careless woman, an alien woman, an ignorant woman, a sinful woman, a disreputable woman, a hardened woman, an avoided woman—yet a religious woman. And many "believed on Him [Jesus] because of the word of the woman who testified" (John 4:39, ASV).

One is tempted to dwell upon Jesus' step-by-step winning of this soul to Himself. Our chief point in this study, however, is to note how God in this instance used "the word of the woman" to win a host of souls to "the Saviour of the world" (John 4:39-42).

The disciples had gone away to nearby Sychar to purchase food. When they returned, they "marvelled" that Jesus "talked with the woman" (John 4:27) for this was entirely contrary to rabbinic precepts. They had all been taught that the Jewish oral law should be burned rather than taught to a woman. In fact, there were several reasons why the disciples marvelled that Jesus should be engaged in earnest conversation with this woman.

> First, they wondered that He . . . talked with her because she was only a woman. Second, because she was a Samaritan woman with whom no Jew should have dealings. Third, because she was a sinner. Some versions speak of her a "*the* woman of Samaria," and she was likely well-known because of her association with men.[6]

After meeting Christ and becoming convicted of her need of the living water, she "left her waterpot, and went her way into the city, and saith to the men, 'Come, see a man, which told me all things that ever I did: Is not this the Christ?' " (John 4:28-29) Thus from this newly converted soul there began to flow forth living water. She left her water jar, for she had the living water springing up within. What need did she have for the old waterpot?

This witnessing woman spread abroad what she had discovered about the Messiah and the worship of God, and she invited her listeners to "come and see" for themselves. A number of them did so with this blessed result: "Many of the Samaritans of that city believed on Him for the saying of the woman, which testified, 'He told me all that ever I did' " (John 4:39). This witness by a woman was indeed a potent, public testimony concerning the Saviour, a word which God blessed to the salvation of men. Surely then there is no reason why women, when God calls them, should not openly testify concerning the Gospel today.

Mary of Bethany

"Now when Jesus was in Bethany, in the house of Simon the leper, there came unto Him a woman having an alabaster box of very precious ointment, and poured it on His head, as He sat at meat" (Matt. 26:6-7). This woman was Mary of Bethany (John 12:1-3). Apparently she was the only person among our Lord's disciples who had grasped the significance of His frequently repeated declarations of His death and resurrection. When someone objected to the alleged waste of the costly ointment, Christ replied,

> In that she hath poured this ointment on My body, she did it for My burial. Verily, I say unto you, wheresoever this Gospel shall be preached in the whole world, there shall also this, that this woman hath done, be told for a memorial of her. (Matt. 26:12-13)

Here indeed was a noble action, a kind of public testimony not in words but in act, something no man among the disciples had discerned, much less thought of doing. By this public ministry Mary proclaimed to all the world the good news of the sacrifice the Lamb of God was about to make.

Caring Women

In Luke's Gospel we read of women who followed our Lord in His journeys: "certain women, which had been healed of evil spirits and infirmities, Mary called Magdalene, out of whom went seven devils, and Joanna the wife of Chuza Herod's steward, and Susanna, and many others, which ministered unto Him of their substance" (Luke 8:2-3). Deeply devoted to the Saviour, these women staunchly supported him, even to the meeting of His material needs; and they did this in spite of the fact that He was facing growing criticism and fierce opposition from His adversaries.

In his *Expository Thoughts on the Gospel of Luke* the great Bishop J.C. Ryle commented on this passage:

> We can well imagine that the difficulties these holy women had to face in becoming Christ's disciples were neither few nor small. They had their full share of contempt and scorn which was poured on all followers of Jesus by the Scribes and Pharisees. They had, besides, many a trial from the hard speeches and hard usage which any Jewish woman who thought for herself about religion would probably have to undergo. But none of these things moved them. Grateful for mercies received at our Lord's hands, they were willing to endure much for His sake. Strengthened inwardly by the renewing power of the Holy Ghost, they were enabled to cleave to Jesus and not give way. And nobly they did cleave to Him to the very end.[7]

Daughters of Jerusalem

"And there were following Him a great multitude of the people, and of women who were mourning and lamenting Him" (Luke 23:27, NASB). According to Dr. James Stalker,

> The Galilean men who had surrounded Him in His hour of triumph put in no appearance now in His hour of despair; but the women of Jerusalem broke away from the example of the men and paid the tribute of tears to His youth, character and sufferings. It is said that there was a Jewish law forbidding the showing of any sympathy to a condemned man; but, if so, this demonstration was all the more creditable to those who took part in it. The upwelling of their emotion was too sincere to be dammed back by barriers of law and custom.[8]

The doom of Jerusalem was nigh at hand—a doom almost unparalleled in the history of suffering humanity. Foreseeing this horror, Jesus on the eve of His own unspeakable sufferings said to the women who followed Him, "Daughters of Jerusalem, weep not for Me, but weep for yourselves, and for your children" (Luke 23:28). These words, uttered in such an extremity, reveal His tender consideration for women and children. "The tears of the women displayed a sympathy and an appreciation for Him such as the men were incapable of," and His words to them revealed "a sympathy with them, such as had never before existed in the world"⁹ that down-grades the weaker sex.

Let us remember that in those days women as well as slaves were often considered so inferior as to be but burden-bearing pieces of property with no rights whatever to equality with men. While that ancient world was a man's world, the Israelite women in the early days enjoyed a status not generally experienced in the East. But Christ brought *full* emancipation to womanhood, and wherever He is recognized and obeyed, woman is esteemed as man's beloved companion.

Dr. Stalker further comments,

It is said there is no instance in the Gospels of a woman being an enemy of Jesus. No woman deserted or betrayed, persecuted or opposed Him. But women followed Him, they ministered to Him of their substance, they washed His feet with tears, they anointed His head with spikenard; and now, when their husbands and brothers were hounding Him to death, they accompanied Him with weeping and wailing to the scene of martyrdom.

It is a great testimony to the character of Christ on the one hand and to that of woman on the other. Woman's instinct told her, however dimly she at first apprehended the truth, that this was the Deliverer for her. Because, while Christ is the Saviour of all, He has been specially the Saviour of woman. At His advent, her degradation being far deeper than that of men, she needed Him more; and wherever His gospel has traveled since then, it has been the signal for her emancipation and redemption. His presence evokes all the tender and beautiful qualities which are latent in her nature; and under His influence her character experiences a transfiguration.[10]

At the Cross

During His dark hour in the Garden of Gethsemane, Christ's disciples "all forsook Him, and fled" (Mark 14:50). When the hounds of hell were closing in on the Lamb in the midst of wolves, no man stood with Him. As Jesus hung on the cross, however, several women stood by. In John's Gospel we read, "Now there stood by the cross of Jesus His mother, and His mother's sister, Mary the wife of Cleophas, and Mary Magdalene" (John 19:25). Mark tells the story as follows:

> There were also women looking on afar off: among whom was Mary Magdalene, and Mary the mother of James the less and of Joses, and Salome; (who also, when He was in Galilee, followed Him, and ministered unto Him;) and many other women which came up with Him unto Jerusalem. (Mark 15:40-41)

Some of these women, sorrowful and perplexed, lingered and watched His burial. "And Mary Magdalene and Mary the mother of Joses beheld where He was laid" (Mark 15:47). A number of these women must have watched through the dark night till the dawn of day. Thank God for the women who watched and waited!

In his *Expository Thoughts on the Gospel of Mark*, Bishop J.C. Ryle comments on the women at the cross:

> Let us notice . . . *what honorable mention is here made of women*. . . . We might well have supposed that, when

all the disciples but one had forsaken our Lord and fled, the weaker and more timid sex would not have dared to show themselves His friends. It only shows us what grace can do. God sometimes chooses the weak things of the world to confound the things that are mighty. The last are sometimes first, and the first last. The faith of women sometimes stands upright, when the faith of men fails and gives way.

But it is interesting to note throughout the New Testament how often we find the grace of God glorified in women, and how much benefit God has been pleased to confer through them on the Church, and on the world.[11]

Referring to the account in Luke, Bishop Ryle points out:

It was *not* a woman who sold the Lord for thirty pieces of silver. They were *not* women who forsook the Lord in the garden and fled. It was *not* a woman who denied Him three times in the high priest's house. But they *were* women who wailed and lamented when Jesus was led forth to be crucified. They *were* women who stood to the last by the cross. And they *were* women who were first to visit the grave "where the Lord lay."[12]

An anonymous poet expressed it this way:

Not she with traitorous lips her Saviour stung;
Not she denied Him with unholy tongue;
She, whilst Apostles shrunk, could danger brave;
Last at the cross, and earliest at the grave.[13]

First Witnesses of the Resurrection

Mary Magdalene was the first to behold the risen Christ and to be commissioned to herald His resurrection. She was sent to declare the grandest news ever proclaimed: "Jesus saith unto her, . . . Go to My brethren, and say unto them, I ascend unto My Father, and your Father; and to My God, and your God" (John 20:17). How quickly she must have sped back to the city to tell the first message from the risen Lord! And would it not seem strange if Christ, who had honored a woman as the first witness to proclaim His good news, should later through Paul's epistles forbid her having any voice in the established church?

Surely the Scriptures clearly show it was to a *woman* that the risen Christ committed His first message in resurrection. "Mary Magdalene came and told the disciples that she had seen the Lord, and that He had spoken these things unto her" (John 20:18). Three times over we find Mark describing the unbelief of the eleven disciples: "And they, when they had heard that He was alive, and had been seen of her, believed not" (Mark 16:11). Again when Christ had appeared to two of them as they walked, we read, "And they went and told it unto the residue: neither believed they them" (Mark 16:13). Finally when our Lord Himself appeared to them as they sat at meat, "He reproached them for their unbelief and hardness of heart" (Mark 16:14, NASB). Although these men had been told repeatedly by our Lord that He would rise again, when the time came, they were "slow of heart to believe." What striking examples of stubborn man's unwillingness to believe that which runs counter to his prejudices!

In the light of the above instances we can see why the Lord so blessed His women followers: He found them ready to believe and to publish to the brethren the resurrection message. What a tribute to these faithful women that at our Lord's resurrection He appeared to them and put their witness of His resurrection at the very heart of His Gospel to be universally proclaimed!

Augustine comments that these women were "the first preachers of the resurrection of Christ." How can we believe that our Lord would choose women to publish to the disciples this most astounding news, and then later put an embargo on their further publishing the glad tidings?

The Great Commission

At the tomb of the risen Lord, the angel's message to Mary
Magdalene, Mary the mother of James, and Salome was: "Go
quickly, and tell His disciples, He is risen from the dead; and
lo, He goeth before you into Galilee; there shall ye see Him"
(Matt. 28:7, ASV). After that our Lord "appeared to above five
hundred brethren at once" (1 Cor. 15:6, ASV), and just before
His ascension He uttered the Great Commission—His missionary mandate for the evangelization of the world:

> Go therefore and make disciples of all the nations,
> baptizing them in the name of the Father and the Son
> and the Holy Spirit, teaching them to observe all that I
> commanded you; and lo, I am with you always, even to
> the end of the age. (Matt. 28:19-20, NASB)

If the question arises whether the *women* were included in
this commission, we can but answer affirmatively that they
were, for we later read that "Saul laid waste the church,
entering into every house, and dragging men and women
committed them to prison" (Acts 8:3, ASV).

> And Saul, yet breathing out threatenings and slaughter
> against the disciples of the Lord, went unto the high
> priest, and desired of him letters to Damascus to the
> synagogues, that if he found any of this way, whether
> they were men or women, he might bring them bound
> into Jerusalem. (Acts 9:1-2)

Some years later he confessed that he had "persecuted this
way unto the death, binding and delivering into prisons both
men and women" (Acts 22:4). It stands to reason that Saul
would not have persecuted the women if they had been silent
persons, not daring to preach "the way" to anyone.

Chapter Six

WOMEN OF THE EARLY CHURCH

L uke records that the disciples who witnessed the ascension of the Lord Jesus "returned to Jerusalem with great joy; and were continually in the temple, blessing God" (Luke 24:52-53, ASV). This joyful company likely included women, for they were present in the upper chamber where prayer was made continually in preparation for the outpouring of the Spirit on the Day of Pentecost.

> They [the disciples] went up into the upper chamber . . . both Peter and John and James and Andrew, Philip and Thomas, Bartholomew and Matthew, James the son of Alphaeus, and Simon the Zealot, and Judas the son of James. These all with one accord continued stedfastly in prayer, with all the women, and Mary the mother of Jesus, and with His brethren. (Acts 1:13-14, ASV)

Evidently the women joined in prayer with the men and with the brethren of our Lord, now converted. Professor F.F. Bruce suggests that these women "no doubt [included] those who accompanied Jesus from Galilee (Luke 8:2) and those who were present at the Cross and at the grave (Matt. 27:55f; Mark 15:40; 16:1; Luke 24:10; John 19:25)."[1]

Would some expositors dispute the point, insisting that in 1 Timothy 2:8 the Apostle Paul forbids women to join in prayer when men are present? Would they insist that these women merely accompanied the men there and did not themselves join in the prayers? This sounds like the voice of prejudice. To be consistent would they also contend that our Lord's brethren, now believers, merely accompanied the men but did not join in prayer? Bruce further states, "It is significant that she [Mary, the mother of Jesus] is found in prayer with His disciples."[2]

The Day of Pentecost

In Acts 2:1, 4 we read that "they were all with one accord in one place," and "they were all filled with the Holy Ghost, and began to speak with other tongues, as the Spirit gave them utterance." This supernatural manifestation confounded and astonished the crowd of devout Jews who were assembled in Jerusalem from every quarter of the Roman Empire. When they heard the disciples, evidently both men and women, speaking in their various languages the "wonderful works of God," they asked, "What meaneth this?" But the unbelieving Jews of Jerusalem, mocking, charged the disciples with drunkenness (Acts 2:11-12). In the midst of the confusion the Apostle Peter lifted up his voice and spoke to them.

Ye men of Judea, and all ye that dwell at Jerusalem, be this known unto you, and give ear unto my words. For these are not drunken, as ye suppose; seeing it is but the third hour of the day; but this is that which hath been spoken through the prophet Joel: And it shall be in the last days, saith God, I will pour forth of My Spirit upon all flesh: and your sons and your daughters shall prophesy, and your young men shall see visions, and your old men shall dream dreams: yea and on My servants and on My handmaidens in those days will I pour forth of My

Spirit: and they shall prophesy. . . . And . . . whosoever shall call on the name of the Lord shall be saved. (Acts 2:14-21, ASV)

In his sermon Peter did not imply that Pentecost was the ultimate fulfillment of Joel's prophecy (Joel 2:28-31), for that still awaits further fulfillment in the coming "last days." Instead he conveyed the idea that "this is that Spirit of which Joel spoke," a kind of *foretaste* of the Spirit's falling upon a righteous Israel—that which will yet take place at the end of the age, "the last days," culminating in that "great and notable day of the Lord" (Acts 2:20; Joel 2:31). At that time all ungodliness shall be purged away and the Spirit shall be poured out on a wholly righteous nation.

Yes, Peter definitely related the Pentecostal outpouring to that ancient prophecy of Joel when the prophet foretold that the Spirit would be outpoured without restriction and without distinction of race or sex. "Your sons and your daughters shall prophesy. . . . Yea and on My servants and on My handmaidens in those days will I pour forth of My Spirit; and they shall prophesy" (Acts 2:17-18, ASV). So the Spirit-anointed daughters and handmaidens, as well as sons and bondmen, were to give out the Gospel and declare the wonderful works of God "as the Spirit gave them utterance." Issuing from Pentecost, their messages would center around what God had recently done for sinful humanity through the death and resurrection of Christ.

In light of the above facts can we think for a moment that women were kept in silence in the early days of the church? Surely not. According to the Scriptures the preaching of the Gospel after Pentecost was done not only by the apostles but by scattered church members manifestly inclusive of both sexes. In a sense this was the first lay movement of the Christian church. If women had been forbidden to speak or confess openly, as they were customarily denied liberty to speak in the synagogues of that day, they would not have been persecuted. Women must have been preaching the

Word, for they as well as the men drew down the fiery persecution that committed them to prison. And there is no carefully worded footnote to indicate that they confined their preaching to "sisters' meetings."

The Book of Acts portrays a number of devout and honorable women of the early church; in fact some thirty-three are mentioned. In Jerusalem, Samaria, Joppa, Damascus, Philippi, Thessalonica, Berea, and Athens women disciples were among the first members of the churches, and they had a vital part in church activities.

> If we look into the history of the Primitive Church we shall find that women laboured very abundantly in the Gospel. . . . After the disciples were engaged in preaching the Gospel to all nations, we find from the annals of Christianity that they were among the most constant and devoted fellow-labourers of the Apostle Paul and his compeers.[3]

In the words of Dwight M. Pratt,

> Women were prominent, from the first, in the activities of the early church. . . . Women, as truly as men, were recipients of the charismatic gifts of Christianity. The apostolic greetings in the epistles, give them a place of honor. [To] the church at Rome . . . [Paul] sends greetings to at least eight [women] prominent in Christian activity . . . (Romans 16:1, 3, 12, 15).
>
> It is evident in the New Testament and in the writings of the Apostolic Fathers that women . . . were assigned official duties in the conduct and ministrations of the early church.[4]

Many of these women were persecuted (by such as Saul of Tarsus) and suffered much for their faith. Among the many references to outstanding women in the New Testament after Pentecost, we shall note just a few.

Dorcas

In the seacoast town of Joppa lived a disciple called Dorcas. This honorable woman, "full of good works and almsdeeds," was well known and respected for her incessant ministry to the poor and needy. At her deathbed the weeping widows were showing the garments she had made; then God through Peter raised her from the dead, and many believed in the Lord (Acts 9:36-42).

Lydia

Lydia was a successful businesswoman and charter member of the church at Philippi. In Acts 16:13-15 we read of the beginning of this church:

> On the Sabbath day we [Paul and his companions] went forth without the gate by a river side, where we sup-posed there was a place of prayer; and we sat down, and spake unto the women that were come together. And a certain woman named Lydia, a seller of purple, of the city of Thyatira, one that worshipped God, heard us: whose heart the Lord opened to give heed unto the things which were spoken by Paul. And when she was baptized, and her household, she besought us, saying, "If ye have judged me to be faithful to the Lord, come into my house, and abide there." And she constrained us. (ASV)

Apparently there was no synagogue in the place, for there were insufficient men to form one. On the Sabbath Paul and his associates went to the "place of prayer," where they spoke to "the women that were come together."

The leading lady was Lydia, a God-fearing Gentile. She was a trader in purple from Thyatira who had evidently become a proselyte of the Jewish faith. The Lord constrained her to give attention to Paul's preaching. She listened, be-lieved, and became the Lord's key servant in Philippi.

Does this seem a strange way for the Gospel to enter
Europe? Perhaps so, but what is more strange is the fact that
Paul was a Pharisee who in his early years had daily repeated
such words as these: "O God, I thank thee I am neither a
Gentile, nor a slave, nor a woman." And before long he
would be writing to the Galatians that in the new creation
"there can be no male and female; for ye all are one man in
Christ Jesus" (Gal. 3:28, ASV). Paul forsook forever the Jewish and pharasaic contempt for women, so he could without
shame or bias speak to the women who were assembled by
the river.

Surprising also is the fact that the open heart of one
woman, Lydia of Philippi, became a foothold for God—the
basis of the Spirit's operations whence proceeded wonderful
Gospel victories. It was but a humble female congregation to
begin with, yet as David Brown comments, "Here . . . were
gathered the firstfruits of Europe unto Christ, and they were
of the female sex."[5]

Euodia and Syntyche

Later in writing to the Philippians Paul mentions other prominent women in that church. He beseeches Euodia and
Syntyche to be "of the same mind in the Lord" (Phil. 4:2);
then Paul entreats a true yokefellow in this way: "Help these
women [Euodia and Syntyche], for they labored with me in
the gospel [*shared my struggle*, lit.]" (Phil. 4:3, ASV). What a
tribute to these women! And what a tragedy to the church if
after having shared Paul's struggle in the cause of the Gospel
they cannot be restored to one another!

Since these women labored with Paul in the Gospel, what
did they do if they did not speak, did not teach, did not
preach? Did they only cook for Paul? Were they allowed only
to minister of their substance with the strict proviso that they
do it "silently"? Surely to labor in the Gospel of good tidings
means to tell something, namely the Good News concerning
the death and burial and resurrection of the Lord Jesus. So

these Philippian women must have proclaimed the Gospel.

Philip's Four Daughters

At Caesarea Paul and his companions stayed in the house of
Philip the evangelist. "Now this man had four virgin daughters who prophesied" (Acts 21:8-9, ASV). As we have seen,
Joel had foretold the outpouring of the Spirit upon daughters
as well as sons; then on the Day of Pentecost Peter had
declared its fulfillment. It may be that Philip and his daughters were present in Jerusalem on the Day of Pentecost and
experienced that marvelous outpouring.

The fact that Philip's four daughters had remained un-
married and were used of God to "prophesy" was a credit to
their godly father's upbringing. One wonders whether they
were mentioned because prophesying was rare or because it
was unusual for four women in one family to do so.

"In ancient Church history the record about Philip's
daughters is that 'they preached Christ where Christ has not
been known!' "[6] The historian Papias tells us "that Philip
and his four daughters later migrated to Asia Minor, and
spent their remaining years in that region, and that the
daughters lived to an advanced age, and were highly esteemed as witnesses of the members and activities of the
early churches of Judea."[7]

Adam Clarke comments,

> Probably these four daughters were no more than *teachers*
> in the Church: for we have already seen that this is a
> frequent meaning of the word *prophesy*; and this is un-
> doubtedly one thing intended by the prophecy of
> Joel. . . . If Philip's daughters might be *prophetesses*,
> why not *teachers?*[8]

That conclusion makes sense.

The account of Philip's daughters presents a problem for
certain expositors who believe that Scripture prohibits wom-

en from any audible public ministry. The question is, how can we explain the action of these four daughters? One commentator suggests that Philip's daughters confined their ministry to women; others speculate about how these daughters must have exercised their prophetic gift to women individually or in private or in meetings in which men were not present. Luke, however, in the Book of Acts mentions in the most matter of fact way the prophesying of these four women. Surely these prophetesses must have had somewhat of a public ministry because nothing is said about any restriction imposed upon them.

Man's attempt to circumvent the clear teaching of Scripture may be likened to a sign over the door of a skillful cabinetmaker's shop: "Here we do all kinds of fancy turnings and twistings." The difficulty with this idea of sisters' meetings is that in all the New Testament there is no hint that in the early churches there were gatherings called sisters' meetings! Often some "fancy turnings and twistings," or at least some fanciful footnotes, are required to make certain Scriptures say what we want them to say. "To claim that these women took public part only in meetings of *women*, is a pitiful recourse to which many have resorted."[9]

To us it seems only reasonable to assume that Philip's daughters exercised their prophetic gift before both men and women. How then can it be essentially wrong for women thus to minister today if they speak under the direction of the same Holy Spirit?

At the close of his letter to the saints at Rome, the Apostle Paul shows his personal regard and high respect for the ministry of Christian women. In the list of greetings he mentions ten women (eight by name), who as his helpers "labored much in the Lord" (Rom. 16:12), boldly facing dangers and persecutions.

Phoebe
Phoebe is the only one classified as a deaconess, but doubt-

less some of the other women had been entrusted with this office. Regarding her, Paul says, "I commend unto you Phoebe our sister, who is a servant [*deaconess*, lit.] of the church that is at Cenchreae" (Rom. 16:1, ASV). Dr. A.J. Gordon comments on the translation of the word *servant* in the above verse:

> The same word, *diakonos*, here translated *servant*, is rendered *minister* when applied to Paul and Apollos (1 Corinthians 3:5), and *deacon* when used of other male officers of the church (1 Timothy 3:10, 12-13). Why discriminate against Phoebe simply because she is a woman? The word *servant* is correct for the general unofficial use of the term, as in Matthew 22:10; but if Phoebe were really a functionary of the Church, as we have a right to conclude, let her have the honor to which she is entitled. If "Phoebe, a minister of the church at Cenchrea" sounds too bold, let the word be transliterated and read, "Phoebe, a deacon"—a deacon, too, without the insipid termination "ess" of which there is no more need than that we should say teacheress or doctoress. . . . It is wonderful how much there is in a name! "Phoebe, a servant" might suggest to an ordinary reader nothing more than the modern church drudge who prepares sandwiches and coffee for an ecclesiastical sociable. To Canon Garrett, with his genial and enlightened view of women's position in apostolic times, "Phoebe, a deacon" suggests a useful co-laborer of Paul "travelling about on missionary and other labors of love."[10]

Rotherham, an honest-minded Plymouth brother, translates the passage, "Phoebe . . . being a minister of the Assembly which is at Cenchrea."

Bishop Lightfoot once said, "As I read my New Testament the theme is clear that a female diaconate is as definite an institution in the Apostolic Church as the male diaconate.

Phoebe is as much a deacon as Stephen or Philip is a deacon."[11]

Katherine Bushnell refers to Bishop Lightfoot's stand on this issue:

> [He] speaks of the mistranslation "servant" in this place. He also gives strong reasons for believing that 1 Timothy 3:11 refers also to woman deacons, and adds: "If the testimony borne in these two passages [Romans 16:1, and 1 Timothy 3:11] to a ministry of women in the Apostolic times had not thus been blotted out of our English Bibles . . . our English church would not have remained so long maimed of one of her hands."[12]*

From a secular and very ancient source comes the testimony of Pliny the Younger (A.D. 62–113). As governor of the province of Bithynia, he wrote to the Roman Emperor Trajan for advice regarding the persecution of Christians because so many of all classes were turning to Christ. Here is part of Pliny's letter:

> I thought it the more necessary to inquire into the real truth of the matter by subjecting to torture two female slaves who were called "deacons," but I found nothing more than a perverse superstition which went beyond all bounds. Therefore, I deferred further inquiry in order to apply to you for a ruling . . . because of the number of those who were accused. For many of every age, every class, and of both sexes are being accused.[13]

Did not Pliny choose these two "female slaves" to torture because they, like Phoebe, held some official position as

---

*The marginal reading of 1 Timothy 3:11 in the NIV is "In the same way deaconesses."

deacons and could reveal what Christianity was all about? Pliny also refers to these Christian deacons in these words: "maidservants who are called female ministers."[14] So we have clear evidence within and without Scripture for the existence of women deacons, or ministers, from early times.

Concerning Phoebe, Paul continues, "that ye receive her in the Lord, as becometh saints, and that ye assist her in whatsoever business she hath need of you: for she hath been a succourer of many, and of myself also" (Rom. 16:2). The word translated "succourer" or "helper" occurs no other place in the New Testament, but is the feminine form of the Greek word *prostatēs* (Latin *patronus*). According to Liddell and Scott's lexicon the literal meaning is "one who stands before, front-rank man, leader, chief, protector, champion."[15]

> Phoebe was therefore obviously a woman of means and position and may have acted as Paul's "patron." He was . . . asking the men and women believers in Rome to "stand by" her, to be at her disposal in any way she required, since she had "stood forth" as a leader or supervisor. It is the same kind of consideration he asks for other church leaders and elders in 1 Thessalonians 5:12-13 and 1 Timothy 5:17.[16]

W.J. Conybeare says of Phoebe: "She was a widow of consideration and wealth, who acted as one of the deaconesses of the Church, and now was about to sail to Rome, upon some private business, apparently connected with a lawsuit in which she was engaged."[17] Evidently Paul had committed to Phoebe the delivery of his Epistle to the Romans.

Dorothy Pape writes:

> This important theological statement about sin and salvation addressed to the believers in the prestigious capital city was entrusted to . . . Phoebe, who carried it the several hundred miles from Corinth to Rome—an arduous, even dangerous journey in those days. And some

consider this "a responsibility only given to someone of
official standing."[18]

Priscilla

After Phoebe, Paul greets "Priscilla and Aquila, my helpers in
Christ Jesus" (Rom. 16:3). The order here is significant: the
woman's name appears first as in four out of six places in the
New Testament when properly translated.

Note this pertinent comment from a scholarly
commentator:

> The frequent sneers at Paul about his view respecting
> the female sex and their prerogatives might be spared
> us, were this chapter carefully read. The order here is a
> sufficient answer: The wife's name first, because she
> was foremost, no doubt. The standard is, after all, ca-
> pacity, not sex. Both are called "my helpers," and it
> would seem that, as such, they were both engaged in
> spiritual labours, which term includes vastly more than
> public preaching.[19]

Continuing, Paul testifies of Priscilla and Aquila that they
risked "their own necks" to save him, and all the Gentile
churches owe them a great debt as "helpers" in spiritual
ministry (Rom. 16:4). The word that is rather weakly translated "helpers" in the *King James Version* of Romans 16:3 is
translated "workfellow" and "fellowlabourer" when applied
to Timothy (Rom. 16:21; 1 Thess. 3:2) and to other men
(Phile. 24). Adolf von Harnack says that the Greek word
means literally "fellow-workers in Christ Jesus" and "signifies they were professional evangelists and teachers."[20]

Other Women Saints

Next to be greeted is Mary, "who bestowed much labour on
us" (Rom. 16:6), then Andronicus and Junia, "my kinsmen

and my fellow-prisoners, who are of note among the apostles, who also were in Christ before me" (Rom. 16:7). We are not sure if Junia is a feminine name, but this view is commonly held. Chrysostom, who as a Greek father in the fourth century ought to be taken as a high authority, makes this frank comment on the passage: "Oh, how great is the devotion of this woman, that she should be even counted worthy of the appelation of apostle!"[21] So this great church father regarded this lady as one of the apostolic order of that day. Since we have already seen Phoebe named among the deacons, we should not be surprised that a woman is mentioned among the apostles.

Tryphena and Tryphosa, apparently female slaves, were hailed for their "labour in the Lord" (Rom. 16:12). Persis "laboured much in the Lord," perhaps unceasingly or for a long time. And we should also note the delicate mention of "the beloved Persis." In speaking of men Paul says, "my beloved" (Rom. 16:5, 8-9); he now carefully omits the pronoun *my* before this woman's name.

"Salute Rufus chosen in the Lord, and his mother and mine" (Rom. 16:13). Paul calls Rufus "chosen in the Lord," which in a sense is true of all saints. But perhaps Rufus is thus mentioned because of some tender service which the mother of Rufus rendered to God's itinerant servants, such as Paul. Had the Apostle Paul left all for Christ? Had he now found a "mother" indeed in this saintly woman? What a privilege for this unnamed woman to be considered by the great apostle as a mother to him! What an opportunity for other mother hearts to exercise gracious care for Gospel laborers in all the world!

In Romans 16:14 Paul mentions five names of "brethren," but in verse 15 he mentions five more "saints" who include two women, one named Julia. He speaks here not of brethren, but of saints, since this term can include both sexes.

The number of women Paul mentions in this list shows the high honor and prominence placed upon womanhood by the early church. This large proportion of women's names is all the more significant when we recall the menial place women occupied in the social life at that time.

One might wonder what work of the Lord these women so worthily accomplished. Of what did their "labor" consist? In Philippians 4:3 Paul exhorts, "Help those women which laboured with me [*shared my struggle*, NASB] in the gospel." Did these "labour in the gospel" under the sweeping restriction that they should not *preach* the Gospel? Did they labor in the Lord under a sacred bondage to give no public witness for the Lord? Was theirs not a spiritual ministry? It is difficult to believe that their labor was meant to consist only of sandwiches and silence. Surely these women must have been active in Gospel ministry, and the men must have been exhorted to rally to their "help."

Such free and bold mention of worthy women illustrates the large share borne by them in the early propagation of the faith and the upbuilding of the church. Their responsibility and enterprise in spreading the Gospel stand in striking contrast to the generally degraded condition of women in those days. The number of such women in the early church might well be expanded to include Apphia (Phile. 2), Claudia (2 Tim. 4:21), "of the chief women not a few," and "honourable women which were Greeks" (Acts 17:4, 12). Nor can one overlook Lois and Eunice, grandmother and mother of Timothy, whose ceaseless teaching of the Holy Scriptures gave the great apostle his most trusted assistant in the ministry (2 Tim. 1:5; 3:15).

All through the ages churches have been greatly indebted to their women. As Dr. F.B. Meyer comments, "Many of them [churches] must have been disbanded if holy women had not bound them together by their presence and their prayer. Think of all the children like Chrysostom—'golden-mouthed'—who have been reared by Christian mothers; of all the hymns in our hymnbooks we owe to women."[22] Little do we realize how much of our Christian heritage springs from women's ministry!

Chapter Seven

"NO MALE AND FEMALE"

I n Galatians 3:28 we read, "There can be neither Jew nor Greek, there can be neither bond nor free, there can be no male and female; for ye all are one man in Christ Jesus" (ASV). After the lapse of many centuries, this great apostolic saying has now yielded up its fuller meaning and blessing.

William Barclay reminds us that every Jewish male was taught to thank God daily that "God had not made him 'a Gentile, a slave, or a woman.' "[1] Having this tradition in mind, Paul declares that these categories, with their contrasted privileges and priorities which had long existed in the world of fallen humanity, have been done away in Christ. Concerning these traditions, which have enslaved women for centuries, Edward and James Hastings make this comment: "It has taken a long time in the case of . . . two great relationships—those of class and sex—to cast down the barriers."[2]

Few have been the translators or commentators who have noted the exact wording of the third clause of Galatians 3:28: "there can be no male and female." In careful exegesis this wording becomes significant. Most English versions inaccurately show Paul's declaration to the Galatians: "There is neither Jew nor Greek, there is neither bond nor free, there is neither male nor female." Translators have failed to note the importance of the precise wording of "male and female." (The NASB gives this rendering, but only in the margin.) According to Richard and Joyce Boldrey, "the series 'neither . . . nor' has been interrupted by the use of '*and*,' suggesting that the better translation of the verse would be,

> "There is neither Jew nor Greek,
> There is neither slave nor free,
> There is no 'male and female'—
> For all of you are one
> In Christ Jesus."[3]

Fausset also brings out the significance of "and" in "no male and female."

[The literal Greek reads] "There is *not* male *and* female." Alterable social distinctions are contrasted by "neither . . . nor:" the unalterable human one of sex, by "and" (Mark 10:6). Male and female form a unity, the one supplementing the other. There is no distinction, spiritually, into male and female. Difference of sex makes no difference in Christian privileges. But under the law the male had great privileges. Males alone had in their body circumcision, the sign of the covenant, (whereas *baptism* applies to male and female alike); they alone were capable of being kings and priests, whereas all of either sex are now "kings and priests unto God" (Rev. 1:6); they had prior right to inheritances. In the resurrection the relation of the sexes shall cease (Luke 20:35).[4]

Not only are all distinctions of social caste or religious rank swept away in Christ but even the natural distinction of sex is banished in the new creation. According to the Boldreys, "In Christ, relationships between men and women should transcend the male-female division. . . . For men and women, this implies that the war between the sexes is over."[5]

Throughout the New Testament we find a harmonizing of sexes, a balance,

> a realization of the complementary qualities of male and female. This balance between the sexes is to be found throughout the Gospels: the song of Mary is followed by the song of Zacharias. Both Simeon and Anna welcome the Infant Jesus in the Temple. The conversation with Nicodemus is followed by Jesus' conversation with the Samaritan woman (John 3 and 4). Peter's great confession (John 6:69) is balanced by Martha's "Lord: I believe that thou are the Christ, the Son of God" (John 11:27). Women as well as men accompanied Jesus on His journeys. In the synagogue the man with the withered hand and the woman bowed with an infirmity were both made whole on the Sabbath [Luke 6:6-10; 13:10-13]. . . . Jesus in His teaching, addressed Himself to both men and women.[6]

Were it not for the Christ of Christianity, women of all lands where the Gospel is utterly unknown might still be classed as slaves and idiots.

Chapter Eight

WOMAN'S RIGHT TO PROPHESY

B efore we consider woman's right to prophesy, let us first clarify the meaning of the word *prophesy*. In the New Testament, to prophesy "signifies not merely to foretell future events, but to communicate religious truth in general under a divine inspiration."[1]

While not limited to the revelation of future events, prophecy does often bear this usage in the Bible. For instance in the New Testament we read, "There came down from Judea a certain prophet, named Agabus." This man prophesied that Paul would be bound at Jerusalem (Acts 21:10-11). And again, "Enoch, the seventh from Adam, prophesied . . . 'the Lord is coming' " (Jude 14-15, NIV).

In its general biblical usage, however, *prophecy* is linked with the declaration of God's truth—His will and purpose. For example, God made Aaron a prophet to convey what Moses received directly from the Lord:

And the Lord said unto Moses, "See, I have made thee a god to Pharaoh; and Aaron thy brother shall be thy prophet. Thou shalt speak all that I command thee: and Aaron thy brother shall speak unto Pharaoh, that he send the children of Israel out of his land." (Ex. 7:1-2)

A true prophet, then, is one so in communication with God as to be able to reveal His mind and will to others.

The Prophetess Anna had been giving public testimony long before the occasion when she spoke of the infant Messiah in the temple (Luke 2:36-38). She prophesied, that is, she delivered God's message, to all the assembled crowds who were looking for the Redeemer. With her gift of prophecy she taught others.

In 1 Corinthians 11:4-5 Paul sanctions the right of women as well as men to pray and prophesy: "Every man who prays or prophesies with his head covered dishonors his head. And every woman who prays or prophesies with her head uncovered dishonors her head" (NIV). How else are we to understand Paul here if he is not implying that women normally participate in public prayer and prophecy? Surely he would not explain the *how* of doing that which was not permitted. Commentator Adam Clarke has well said:

> Whatever may be the meaning of *praying* and *prophesying* in respect to the *man*, they have precisely the same meaning in respect to the *woman*. So that some women, at least, as well as some men, might speak to others to *edification*, and *exhortation* and *comfort*. [1 Cor. 14:3, 31] And this kind of prophesying or teaching was predicted by Joel, 2:28, and referred to by Peter, Acts 2:17. And had there not been such gifts bestowed on *women*, the prophecy could not have had its fulfillment.[2]

Dr. Clarke's interpretation makes simple, scriptural common sense, for if Paul's words do not imply that women did actually pray and prophesy in the church at that time, surely his language has no meaning. And if he does not sanction their right to pray and to prophesy by prescribing proper appearance while so engaged, we do not know what to make of his statements.

Another author comments, "The question with the Corinthians was not whether or not the woman should pray or prophesy at all; that question had been settled on the day of Pentecost [Acts 2:17-18]; but whether as a matter of convenience, they might do so without their veils."[3] The Apostle, therefore, is simply explaining that by the law of nature and the custom of that society it would be out of order for her to uncover her head in public worship. To us it is plain that women's participation in public praying and prophesying is a practice quite in harmony with the great body of biblical truth.

Custom and Order

In order to understand Paul's teaching on the public ministry of women, we must know something of the social, cultural, and religious background of the people addressed in his epistles. In writing to the Corinthians, Paul mentions the need for a woman to have her head covered when praying or prophesying (1 Cor. 11:5-6, 13-15).

In Paul's day women customarily wore a veil, or head covering, when appearing in public in the presence of men. The admonition here applies to the cultural setting of that time, not necessarily to women universally in all ages. The fact that he refers to tradition, nature, and custom and bids his readers, "Judge for yourselves" (1 Cor. 11:13, NASB), seems to be just grounds for regarding his instructions here as not binding on us or on all believers for all time.

[In 1 Corinthians 11:2-16 it is evident that] Paul is correcting the hasty impressions that the new believers were receiving regarding their positions as Christians. A flood of new ideas was suddenly poured in upon their minds [as new converts], one of which was the equality of all before God and of a Saviour for all alike. There was neither Jew nor Greek, male nor female, etc. now. And it dawned on the woman that she was neither man's

toy nor slave, but that she had a life to frame for herself.
She was not dependent upon men for her Christian
privileges; ought she not to show this by laying aside the
veil, which was the acknowledged badge of dependence? [But] among the Greeks [and other areas of the
Near East] it was the universal custom for the women to
appear in public with the head covered. . . . It was the
one significant rite in marriage that she assumed the veil
in token that now her husband was her head.[4]

The temptation of the Corinthian women was to carry their
new liberties too far. Paul would caution them to "take heed
lest by any means this liberty of yours become a stumbling-
block" (1 Cor. 8:9). In *The Speaker's Bible* we have the following assessment of the situation:

[The early church's] inherited prejudices were fortified
. . . by a very natural fear of scandal attaching to the
infant community. That this fear was not groundless we
see from the Apostles' writings. For this great and rapid
elevation of womanhood, on the principle that "in
Christ Jesus there can be no male nor female," did not
take place without incidental disorders. . . . Those
which are noticed in the Epistles of St. Paul are dealt
with by him according to circumstances of time and
place, yet on general principles. They occurred principally among the excitable and licentious population of
Corinth. There the gift of prophecy, exercised by wom-
en at and after Pentecost (as in the case of Philip's
daughters), was in danger of becoming discredited by
some who, when praying or prophesying, cast off the
veil.[5]

Apparently some of the Christian women of Corinth
claimed equality in every respect with men and the right to
appear and act as men did. Equality of believers they had a
right to claim, but they were forgetting their subjection in

regard to order, modesty, and propriety.

> This movement of the Corinthian women Paul meets by
> reminding them that personal equality is perfectly con-
> sistent with social subordination. The woman must not
> argue that because she is independent of her husband in
> the greater sphere she must also be independent of him
> in the less. [See 1 Cor. 11:4-5.][6]

Whatever Paul had already taught about the spiritual
equality of men and women, he cannot have meant "that
none are to have authority over others. [For the sake of] the
harmony of society there is a gradation of ranks; and social
grievances result, not from the existence of social distinctions, but rather from their abuse."[7] Paul is mainly concerned
here with reverence and order in the church.

The Head-covering
In order to more fully understand the traditional head-cover-
ing required of the Hebrew woman, we must look at 1 Corinthians 11:4-5 more carefully:

> Every man who prays or prophesies with his head cov-
> ered dishonors his head [Christ]. And every woman who
> prays or prophesies with her head uncovered dishonors
> her head [husband]. (NIV)

"These verses are obviously parallel. In the first verse the
Apostle prohibits the man from doing a right thing in a wrong
way, and in the second *he does the same thing*, prohibiting a
woman from doing a right thing in a wrong way."[8]

Paul's first word here is to the man regarding his praying
or prophesying, having his head covered. It was a practice of
Jewish men worshiping in the synagogue to wear a veil (head-
covering) as a mark of guilt and condemnation before God.
Bishop Lightfoot, one of the church's great expositors, has

pointed out that the chief thrust of this passage was to stop
Jewish Christian men from veiling in worship as a mark of
their unworthiness to approach God,

> because the Christian has a righteous standing "in
> Christ," for "there is no condemnation [or unworthi-
> ness] to them that are in Christ Jesus" (Rom. 8:1). For a
> Christian [man] to pray or to prophesy in a Christian
> assembly while still wearing the tallith [a head-covering]
> would be a contradiction of his standing in Christ; it
> would even reflect upon his Head, Jesus Christ.[9]

In 2 Corinthians 3:16 Paul seems to have this in mind when
he writes, "Whenever a man turns to the Lord, the veil is
taken away." (NASB).

In order to understand Paul's words regarding the woman
praying or prophesying with her head unveiled, we must
remember that according to Jewish oral Law a woman was a
sinner if she transgressed the law of Moses or the Jewish
Law. And how does she transgress? "If she appear abroad
with her head uncovered, and if she spins in the streets" and
on through a long list of inhibitions. In fact, there was "the
duty of repudiation of a wife for adultery . . . when she was
seen abroad with her hair 'not done up,' i.e. not covered."[10]

Here is Dr. Adam Clarke's explanation:

> The man had his head *uncovered*, because he was the
> *representative* of Christ; the woman had hers *covered*,
> because she was placed by the order of God in a state of
> subjection to the man, and because it was the *custom*,
> both among the Greeks and Romans, and among the
> Jews an express *law*, that no woman should be seen
> abroad without a veil. This was and is the custom
> through all the east, and none but public prostitutes go
> without veils. And if a woman should appear in public
> without a veil, she would *dishonour her head*—her *hus-
> band*. And she must appear like to those women who

had their hair shorn off as the punishment of whoredom, or adultery.[11]

Commenting on this custom, Dr. Charles Hodge writes,

Dress is in a great degree conventional. A costume which is proper in one country, would be indecorous in another. The principle insisted upon in this paragraph is, that women should conform in matters of dress to all those usages which the public sentiment of the community in which they live demands. The veil in all eastern countries was, and to a great extent still is, the symbol of modesty and subjection. For a woman, therefore, in Corinth to discard the veil was to renounce her claim to modesty, and to refuse to recognize her subjection to her husband. It is on the assumption of this significancy in the use of the veil, that the apostle's whole argument in this paragraph is founded.[12]

Headship—the Order of Creation

In the order of creation man under God has been vested with official headship. This headship does not mean superiority but rather responsibility and order. This order is reflected in the Trinity: Father, Son, and Holy Spirit. All are equal in essence, nature, and dignity; but there needs to be order. From the beginning men and women were endowed with equality, each to be the complement of the other, while at the same time respecting the order of creation and responsibility. As the Apostle Paul states, "The head of every [Christian] man is Christ; and the head of the woman is the man; and the head of Christ is God" (1 Cor. 11:3).

The word *head* in this context evidently denotes a relation both of order and subordination. We are confronted with the relative position of men and women in their relation to one another; yet in their subordination the man submits directly to Christ, and the woman submits both to man and to Christ.

The principle underlying the whole passage is that there is order and subordination in the Godhead as well as in human relationships. The head of the Christian man is Christ; the head of Christ is God; the head of the woman is the man and Christ.

The headship of man over woman is not a matter of superiority and inferiority, any more than the headship of God over Christ is a matter of superiority and inferiority. God (the Father) and Christ (the Son) are one and equal in essence, but in the working out of redemption's plan Christ is subordinate to the Father. This subordination is perfectly consistent with the equality and identity of substance of each Person with the other. Although by nature the Son is equal with God the Father, He is officially in the great redemption subject to Him.

In regard to the relation between Christ and the believer, the latter is, as a member of Christ's body, subordinate to his Head. As to the relation of the man to the woman, though their standing in Christ is the same, the woman is subordinate to the man in the activities of the church and the home. Man's headship is of divine ordering. Woman's subordination is social, not spiritual; and her personal equality is quite consistent with her social subordination.

In 1 Corinthians 11:12 Paul states, "For as the woman is of the man, even so is the man also by the woman; but all things are of God." Hodge comments, "It matters little whether the man was of the woman, or the woman of the man, as both alike are of God."[13] According to the Maréchale: "There is no sex in soul."[14] And Bishop Lightfoot states: "The conventional distinctions of religious caste or of social rank, even the natural distinction of sex, are banished hence. One heart beats in all: one mind guides all: one life is lived by all. Ye are all *one man*, for ye are members of Christ."[15]

Chapter Nine

HARMONIZING 1 CORINTHIANS 11 AND 14

I n 1 Corinthians 14:34-35 Paul gives this admonition:

> Let the women keep silent in the churches; for they are
> not permitted to speak, but let them subject them-
> selves, just as the Law also says. And if they desire to
> learn anything, let them ask their own husbands at
> home; for it is improper [*disgraceful*, mg.] for a woman to
> speak in church. (NASB)

At first glance one might assume that the above verses prohibit women from any speaking in the church; whereas previously in this same letter (1 Cor. 11:4-5), Paul sanctions woman's right to pray and prophesy. In regard to these two
passages in 1 Corinthians, Bible expositors admit that there is
an apparent contradiction. We believe that Scripture does not
oppose Scripture, yet the problem confronts us as to how to
explain this seeming discrepancy.

The question comes to this: which Scripture is the plainer
of the two and should, for this reason, be considered as the
norm of interpretation? One commentator says, "However
the words of this passage are to be understood, no explana-

tion can be admitted that violates the fundamental rule that a plain Scripture should not be set aside because of another not so easily understood."[1] This rule is a good principle to follow in biblical interpretation.

True, there are difficulties in each passage, but the greater difficulty, we believe, is in connection with 1 Corinthians 14:34-35. When we consider this Scripture in its background and context, the meaning "is not so *plain* as some expositors have imagined."[2]

Let us first note that in 1 Corinthians 14 two different Greek words are used for "speaking": *laleō* and *legō*. A careful study of these words will be illuminating.

Though at times the verbs *laleō* and *legō* are used as synonyms, each has its distinctive connotation and much is gained when each is interpreted according to its specific meaning.

Laleō refers to the ability to employ the organs of speech, to give forth an utterance, emit a sound, or express words with the living voice.

Legō means to speak in the sense of declaring an intelligible message. While *laleō* emphasizes the outward form of speech, *legō* refers to the substance and meaning of that which is spoken. . . .

Laleō is ascribed not only to human language, but to the sounds made by animals, to the twittering and chirping of birds, to the humming or buzzing of insects, and to the noise made by inanimate objects like trees, pipes, flutes, and to an echo. . . . *Laleō* is used by the Greeks of the jabbering of infants before they can speak distinctly. The root of the word is *lal*, illustrating the first efforts of a child to talk, as he says la, la, la. . . .

The application of the distinction between *laleō* and *legō* helps clear up an otherwise difficult passage in First Corinthians. We still hear now and then the idea that women are forbidden by Paul to preach the gospel. Advocates of such a view quote 1 Corinthians 14:34-35 in defence of their position.

According to the general context of the New Testament, women are free to pray, witness, exhort, and preach, inasmuch as there is no distinction between men and women regarding salvation and the graces and gifts of the Holy Spirit (Gal. 3:28). Women are included in the commission of world evangelization (Acts 2:17-18). Philip the evangelist had four daughters who were preachers (21:9). To prophesy means to exhort, witness, appeal, preach, according to First Corinthians 14:3. In Romans 16:1-15 is a long list of gospel workers, men and women, some of whom were probably preachers. In Philippians 4:3 Paul says, "Help those women which labored with me in the gospel."

We are certain from Paul's letter itself that the Apostle approved of women preaching, for he implies that the women in the church at Corinth took part in praying and preaching (1 Cor. 11:5). Exactly, therefore, what is Paul saying in 1 Corinthians 14:34-35? In the immediate context there are four keys which unlock the passage: the meaning of the verb, the tense, the situation which called forth the injunction, and the antithetical form of the prohibition.

First, note the verb used. Paul does not use *legō*, but *laleō* which, as we have seen, means primarily to utter sounds, not necessarily intelligible words. It is the . . . idea of la-la-ing.

Second, Paul uses the present infinitive *lalein*, which tense signifies continuous action. According to the force of this infinitive he says, "Let your women keep silence in the churches; for it is not permitted for them to speak (to continue la-la-ing). . . . It is a shame for women to speak (to go on la-la-ing) in the church."

Third, note the situation which called forth the injunction. Why such an exhortation? Because the women were disturbing the church service by asking questions of their husbands during the preaching. In those days education, as always among heathen peoples, was the privilege of the men. As an audience listened with rapt attention to the wonderful gospel, the men with their learning had little difficulty grasping the message. Not so with the women. Hence their questions produced an undertone of noise which was confusing to an audience. No wonder Paul corrected them. So we see that the Apostle is not dealing with the subject of women preaching, but with discipline. He is simply correcting disorder. He had already corrected the men in verses 32-33, "The spirits of the prophets are subject to the prophets. For God is not the author of confusion, but of peace, as in all churches of the saints."

The fourth key is the antithetical form of the prohibition. An antithesis . . . presents two complementary statements, or as we might say, an antithesis has two equal arms. In the injunction of Paul here, one of these arms is prohibitory (vs. 34), and the other is permissive (vs. 35). The permission is: Ask their husbands at home. The prohibition is simply the converse: Don't ask them in church.[3]

In order to rightly interpret 1 Corinthians 14:34-35, we must consider the context, as well as the readers to whom this Scripture was written. New Testament churches, such as the one at Corinth, were made up largely of uneducated, undisciplined Gentile believers; but they also included believing Jews, who were accustomed to the synagogue services with their varied regulations. G.H. Lang gives further insight concerning the background and setting of this crucial passage.

The persons who mostly formed the first churches (as that at Corinth, which is particularly here in question), were not educated, disciplined westerners, to whom routine and decorum (not to say deadness), especially in public worship, have become second nature and seem wholly proper. On the contrary, they were

. . . nervous, restless, emotional . . . impulsive, viva-
cious, talkative; to whom routine was irksome and dul-
ness intolerable. . . . .

Nor had those first believers been trained to a dead-
ly propriety in public services. Their heathen temples
had . . . little semblance of order or sense of
stillness. . . .

Neither was even the synagogue, in which believing
Jews had been reared, marked by the degree of propriety and orderliness to which we in the west are to-day
accustomed in the churches of God. . . . At certain
points of the proceedings extemporary prayers were permitted; also a person desiring to read could rise in his
place and the ruler of the synagogue cause a roll to be
handed to him, and after having read he might address
the congregation (Luke 4:16, 17); or the rulers, seeing
strangers, might invite them to address the people (Acts
13:15). . . . There was much freedom as to entering and
leaving during the service; and in the summer the heat
would cause restlessness, fanning, some leaving for the
outer air and returning. But in addition to these natural
causes of disturbance the Scriptures reveal other fea-
tures. The emotional temperament excited by prejudice
threw a whole congregation into a sudden tumult, with
the alarming accompaniment of the attempted assassina-
tion of the offending teacher (Luke 4:28, 29). We know
(Edersheim, *Sketches*, 276) that if anyone expressed,
even in prayer, what were regarded as false notions he
was immediately stopped, while Acts 13:45 shows the
leaders violently and offensively interrupting Paul while
discoursing, calling forth from him a solemn rejoinder
(46, 47) which last utterance caused an outbreak of
approbation from a section of the audience; an intense
scene, repeated later (18:6). This same oriental excit-
ability caused the uproar in Ephesus among heathen
(ch. 19), and the murderous riot in even the sacred
temple at Jerusalem (ch. 21).[4]

With these conditions in mind it is not too difficult to see that 1 Corinthians 14 was written to correct similar irregularities, common in the church at Corinth, which hindered its activities from being effective "unto edifying" (14:26).

Some persons of the assembly were speaking up but not "in turn" (v. 27). Others were interrupting one another, not giving way to one another (vv. 29-30), with the resulting "confusion." Therefore Paul felt impelled to rebuke this disorderly conduct: "God is not a God of confusion but of peace" (v. 33, NASB).

Now as we look at verse 34, we can easily see how the women in the Corinthian church may have been causing confusion by talking or asking questions. Perhaps they were interrupting the ministry of the assembly during the singing of a psalm, or the teaching of the Word, or the giving of some revelation. Such interruptions would prevent all things being done for edification (v. 26, NASB).

If this is the true explanation of the women "speaking," there is no contradiction whatever between verse 34 and Paul's teaching in 1 Corinthians 11:4-5. Dr. A.H. Strong states that "Paul's injunction to women to keep silence in the churches (1 Cor. 14:35 and 1 Tim., 2:11-12) is to be interpreted by the larger law of gospel equality and privilege (Col. 3:11)."[5] Woman has been freed by the Gospel, and her dignity has been restored.

In conclusion we would register our agreement with Mrs. Needham's comment that in chapter 11 of 1 Corinthians

> . . . the privilege of female praying and prophesying is recognized, honoured, and regulated. In . . . 1 Corinthians 14, it is declared that women shall not *interrupt* the assembly, even for the exercise of these lawful spiritual gifts. "For God is not the author of confusion, but of peace." And He will have men and women preserve order in His holy assembly.[6]

Chapter Ten

SILENCE FOR WOMEN?

F irst Timothy 2:8-15 is usually regarded as perhaps the strongest and most decisive for stopping the mouths of women in the church from either praying or teaching:

> I desire therefore that the men pray in every place, lifting up holy hands, without wrath and disputing. In like manner, that women adorn themselves in modest apparel, with shamefastness and sobriety; not with braided hair, and gold or pearls or costly raiment; but (which becometh women professing godliness) through good works. Let a woman learn in quietness with all subjection. But I permit not a woman to teach, nor to have dominion over a man, but to be in quietness. For Adam was first formed, then Eve; and Adam was not beguiled, but the woman being beguiled hath fallen into transgression: but she shall be saved through her child-bearing, if they continue in faith and love and sanctification, with sobriety. (1 Tim. 2:8-15, ASV)

It may surprise some to find that this portion of Scripture "really contains an exhortation to the orderly and decorous participation of women in public prayer. Yet this is the conclusion of some of the best exegetes."[1]

In verse 8 Paul writes, "I desire that the men pray in every place [presumably place of worship], lifting up holy hands [a customary posture in public prayer], without wrath and disputing." Had some men been displaying "wrath and dissension" (NASB) among themselves in the prayer meeting, thus contradicting the lifting up of "holy hands"? This misbehavior called for a correction by Timothy.

Verse 9 commences with a very emphatic "in like manner." This does not mean "and" or "also" but draws a parallel between what has gone before and what follows. We could cite a number of other Scripture references to show that "in like manner" or "likewise" in New Testament usage expresses a parallel between two or more statements with which it is used. Professor Sir W. Ramsay has observed, "The whole body of women is to be understood as affected by what has been said about the men."[2]

The question comes down to this: How sweeping is the phrase, "in like manner"? Is it a mere connective? Does it refer only to women's dress and deportment, not to the manner in which they should pray publicly? The "I desire" of verse 8 is certainly carried over in thought into verse 9—"I desire that women . . ." And what is it he desires that women should do? Does the passage imply that he would have the "men *pray* in every place," and the women "in like manner" to be *silent*? Where in that case would be the similarity of conduct? Or does the intended likeness lie between the men's "lifting up holy hands" and the women's "adorning themselves in modest apparel" in their public prayers?

The meaning of verses 8 and 9 according to some of the best commentators is simply, "I desire that men pray everywhere, lifting up holy hands. . . . In like manner I desire that women pray in modest apparel." If we let the phrase "in like manner" have its full force in relation to that which precedes, we must well believe that when *men* pray it should be with "holy hands"; when *women* pray their entire appearance should be with modesty. It seems that the parallel here is between men praying with "holy hands," and women praying in a chaste manner. Let us remember that the same Apostle had earlier spoken of women "praying" or "prophesying" in the assembly in a "seemly" manner, "with their heads veiled" [1 Cor. 11:5], and here he implies that they can do so provided they do not adorn themselves in an ostentatious manner which might attract the gaze of the assembly to themselves, and some of them had apparently been doing this. This interpretation certainly harmonizes Paul's teaching in 1 Corinthians 11:5 and this passage in 1 Timothy 2:8-9.[3]

Now we come to verses 11 to 15. This passage is often cited as forbidding oral feminine ministry in the church, but where is the proof that these verses have reference to the *public* exercises of women? An anonymous expositor believes that the reference here is to woman's domestic life rather than to her public behaviour:

After careful consideration [I] have come to the conclusion that this passage is not a continuation of Paul's verses 8-10, but has rather to do [with something new] with the relation between the husband and wife in the home. . . . [My] reasons for [this] view are:

1. There is a sudden change from "women" in the plural to "woman" in the singular in verses 11 and 12, and the Apostle has avoided the use of the article before "woman" in verse 11 (obscured in the AV). If he had been continuing the argument of the preceding verses, he would have written, "Let *the women* learn in quietness with all subjection," that is, in the presence of the "men" already spoken of.

2. Furthermore Paul says that "she [the woman] shall be saved through her child bearing, if they [pre-

sumably the husband and wife] continue in faith and love and sanctification with sobriety (ver. 15)," [or as a footnote in NEB, "if only husband and wife continue in mutual fidelity].[4]

A Christian lawyer affirms this interpretation by stating, "This prohibition refers exclusively to the private life and domestic character of woman, and simply means that an ignorant or unruly woman is not to force her opinions on the man whether he will or no. It has no reference . . . to women sent out to preach the Gospel by the call of the Holy Spirit."[5]

Let me pause here to draw attention to a point which has an important bearing on the meaning of this passage. The Greek makes no distinction between "man" and "husband," the same Greek word being used for both; nor does it distinguish between "woman" and "wife," the same Greek word being used for both. Thus we may translate verses 11 and 12 as follows: "Let a wife learn in quietness with all subjection. But I permit not a wife to teach nor to have dominion over the husband but to be in quietness."

In Martin Luther's German version verse 12 reads, "I permit not a wife to teach nor have dominion over her husband," implying that this is simply a family matter; it has nothing to do with church worship.

To conclude from this verse that a woman is *never* to teach is certainly a distortion of Scripture. Elsewhere Paul intimates that "women may 'teach' in the home, as we see in Titus 2:2-4; but they are not to 'teach' in the sense of 'laying down the law' or 'domineering over' their husbands. In an assembly they may 'pray,' but certainly they are not to 'domineer' there."[6]

George Williams, commenting on verses 11-15, puts it this way:

A married woman (v. 12) was not to teach or to claim authority over her husband but to be in subordination. Many misunderstand this command; they divorce it from its context, which is the family, and they carry it into the prayer-meeting [dealt with in vv. 1-10], and argue that a woman is forbidden to preach or pray—she is not to teach men—not even her dying husband how to escape from the wrath to come! This is a popular error. What God says here is that a wife is not to govern her husband.[7]

Another expositor, J.H. Robinson, says of the passage,

It is primarily an injunction respecting her personal behaviour at home. It stands in connection with precepts respecting her . . . domestic position; especially her relation to her husband. No one will suppose that the Apostle forbids a woman to "teach" absolutely and universally.[8]

When Paul cautioned Timothy that the women should not teach but "be in quietness," evidently he had in mind some who were offensively forward and domineering. We believe the real point of emphasis here is that teaching is not to be delegated to the women unto the point where they assume the authority which rightly belongs to the men. "Man is the head and the teaching is not to be turned over to woman to make her the head. . . . [Paul's caution] is not an order to all women at all times and in all places to refrain from teaching. . . . It is a declaration of the headship of man, . . . and for the purpose of correcting a local condition."[9]

Mr. Robinson further comments,

The "teaching" therefore which is forbidden by the Apostle, is not every kind of teaching any more than, in the previous instance [1 Corinthians 14:34], his prohibition of speaking applied to every kind of speaking in the Church; but it is such teaching as is domineering, and as involves the usurpation of authority over the man. This is the only teaching forbidden by St. Paul in the passage under consideration. . . . [A woman's] teaching may be public, reiterated, urgent, and may comprehend a variety of subjects, provided it be not dictatorial, domineering, nor vociferous; for then, and then only, would it be incompatible with her obedience.[10]

A certain Dr. Taft believes that verse 12 "should be rendered, 'I suffer not a woman to teach *by* usurping authority over the man.' " Taft continues by indicating that "if you accept the idea of a just and equal society where men and women are equally concerned and responsible, you cannot believe that Paul is denying the right of women to teach and pray."[11]

Those who so confidently quote Paul's words "I permit not a woman to teach" as an absolute rule, forbidding a woman to teach and expound spiritual truth, are faced with the noteworthy teaching of Priscilla. This woman "with her husband Aquila, undertook to 'expound the Way of God more carefully' to Apollos, who up to that time 'knew only the baptism of John' (Acts 18:25-26); a man who later became a co-worker with the Apostle Paul (1 Cor. 3:6). Indeed in this ministry of 'expounding the Way of God more carefully' Luke places Priscilla before her husband" [Acts 18:26, in any accurate translation].[12]

Note that the Apostle Paul gives Priscilla the priority in his salutation in Romans: "Greet Priscilla and Aquila, my helpers in Christ Jesus" (Rom. 16:3). See also Acts 18:18 and 2 Timothy 4:19. Evidently Priscilla was the outstanding teacher of the two. In four out of six mentions of this couple, we find that the name of the woman comes first. However, this priority does not mean that she laid down the law in the church, although she must have joined in prayer there and may have exercised the prophetic gift in the assembly.

Silence for Women Only?

What then are we to understand by the word *silence* in

1 Timothy 2:11-12? "Let the woman learn in silence with all subjection. But I suffer not a woman to teach nor to usurp authority over the man, but to be in silence."

Here the translators of the *King James Version* apparently held some biases against women, because the phrase "in silence" should have been translated "in quietness." The *American Standard Version* has corrected this error. If we compare this translation of *silence* with that of 1 Thessalonians 4:11 and 2 Thessalonians 3:12, we find the same word is properly translated in the *King James Version* "quiet" and "quietness." The word means tranquillity, the absence of disturbance, or "desistance from bustle." One scholar says, "Clearly the term does not prohibit all speech, but does call for calm, non-disruptive conduct."[13] The word actually refers not primarily to utterance but rather to deportment.

The injunction to "silence" occurs three times in 1 Corinthians 14—twice to men and once to women. In each case the silence commanded is manifestly conditional rather than absolute and for all time. To man Paul says, "let him keep silence in the church" (v. 28), referring to a man speaking in tongues when there is no interpreter.

Regarding prophets, Paul writes, "Let two or three prophets speak," with the condition that "if a revelation be made to another who is seated, let the first keep silent" (vv. 29-30, NASB). Paul is not meaning that these men remain forever silent, but that they simply refrain from any speaking that causes confusion. To our knowledge no expositor has ever taught that Paul meant to impose upon men more than a temporary silence.

Then follows the injunction: "Let the women keep silent in the churches" (v. 34, NASB). This exhortation is manifestly given to prevent women from interrupting the service by asking questions, since Paul adds, "for they are not permitted to speak . . . and if they desire to learn anything, let them ask their own husbands at home" (vv. 34-35, NASB). Paul is simply correcting the disorder and confusion in the church. He is dealing, not with the public exercise of spiritual gifts in the pulpit, but with persons in the congregation. He is refer-ring not to women speakers or evangelists in the pulpit but to women interrupters causing confusion in the pew.

At Corinth the church was characterized by noisy tumult rather than solemn worship. There was general pandemoni-um, wranglers speaking out of turn—shameful indeed among men, but more particularly among the women. Some may wonder, "Why did not Paul also say that it was shameful for *men* to speak in the churches? Would this not be just as disturbing as if the *women* did so?" The reason is obvious: men were not so addicted as women to this disturbing prac-tice of talking in the church. A missionary from Asia once commented, "In China, the women are so talkative that for once that we have to tell the men to be silent, we have to tell the women a dozen times, but we do not mean thereby that they are not to sing, pray, or exhort as the Spirit leads them."[14]

Here in the Grecian world reputable women were seen—not heard—when in public, particularly in the presence of men. So these noisy Corinthian women were in danger of bringing disgrace, not only upon their own sex but also upon the cause of Christ. Paul therefore dealt drastically with the shameful conduct of the women. He thought it necessary to reprove all disorderly conduct, especially disorderly speech.

Dorothy Pape notes that Frederik Franson, great mission-ary leader and founder of what is now The Evangelical Alliance Mission (TEAM), searched both the Old and New Testaments for every reference to any kind of speaking ministry or responsible position of women. He came up with the conclusion that there are nearly one hundred such refer-ences in the Bible.[15] This is all the more remarkable in view of the fact that there are but two or three references which seem to be against women's audible ministry. Yet these few references have been made the basis for muzzling women in spite of the fact that the main thrust of Scripture is against such silencing.

Mrs. George C. Needham raises the following question:

Upon what ground . . . should the silence laid upon the
women be distorted and elevated into so much greater
prominence than it bears in reference to the men? No-
body argues that these commands enforced upon the
Corinthian men everlasting cessation from public prayer,
and praise, and preaching. . . . The Apostle expressly
guards his words from misapprehension by explaining,
"Ye *all* may prophesy, ONE BY ONE!" [1 Cor. 14:31,
italics and capitalization hers][16]

A.H. Strong voices the same sentiment when he says,

Paul's injunction to women to keep silence in the
churches (1 Cor. 14:35; 1 Tim. 2:11, 12) is to be interpreted by the larger law of gospel equality and privilege
(Col. 3:11). Modesty and subordination once required a
seclusion of the female sex which is no longer obliga-
tory. Christianity has emancipated woman and has restored her to the dignity which belonged to her at the
beginning.[17]

If the minimal mention of Paul's "silence" to women is
set up as a scriptural command for all time, what is to be done
with the many other commands of Scripture which open the
mouths of women as well as men?

"Praise ye the Lord" (repeated nearly one hundred
    times in Psalms alone).
"Declare among the people His doings" (Ps. 9:11).
"Make a joyful noise unto God" (Ps. 66:1).
"Talk ye of all His wondrous works" (Ps. 105:2).
"Let the redeemed of the Lord say so" (Ps. 107:2).
"Let every thing that hath breath praise the Lord" (Ps.
    150:6).
"Speaking to one another in psalms and hymns and
    spiritual songs . . . always giving thanks for all
    things" (Eph. 5:19-20, NASB).

"Holding forth the word of life" (Phil. 2:16).
"Teaching and admonishing one another in psalms and
   hymns and spiritual songs" (Col. 3:16).

What worthy expositor would claim that these commands and exhortations were meant for men only?

Let's Be Consistent

Carried to its logical conclusion, the *absolute silence* doctrine for women would exclude all female voices in church music, whether solo or ensemble. Professor F.F. Bruce has rather dryly remarked, "I have never known a company in which 1 Corinthians 14:34 ['Let your women keep silence in the churches'] was taken so literally as to impose absolute silence: if Christian women kept silence in the churches while their menfolk sang, the result would be less tuneful singing than we are accustomed to."[18] But in the days of the celebrated musician Johann Sebastian Bach, women *were* prohibited from singing hymns in the German church on the basis of this same verse.

One of our own graduates with a beautiful singing voice has recently been brought under this bondage of silence. At one time she had a fruitful ministry in song, but now she feels obligated to follow the silence doctrine to the extreme and refrain from all public singing. What a tragedy!

How great would be the loss should we eliminate from our hymnbooks all selections by women songwriters! As we think of songs written by Fanny Crosby, Frances Ridley Havergal, and others that have been sung throughout the world, we can but praise God for the glorious public ministry these songwriters have had. Who would want to cast a ballot to exclude these hymns and spiritual songs from our Gospel worship services? Who would want to silence the voice of Charlotte Elliott and her great evangelistic hymn, "Just As I Am"? And what about the many women in those groups where they are denied a public voice? How can they sincerely sing with Frances Ridley Havergal, "Take my voice and let me sing"?

Our appeal is for consistency. The Scripture says, "Let your women keep silence in the churches." If we insist upon literal, legalistic interpretation, let us then eliminate all women teachers in Sunday School, Bible school, and in schools and churches on the mission field! Such women are not keeping silence; neither are they literally fulfilling the order "I permit not a woman to teach" (1 Tim. 2:12).

Perhaps on no subject more than the present one has there been greater bondage to "the letter that killeth." Men have persistently and unreasonably and stubbornly—with little warrant and less logic—contended against a woman's voice in public, using principally 1 Corinthians 14:34 and 1 Timothy 2:11-12.

What right has any man to direct either of these isolated Scriptures against the woman who performs any ministry in the church that causes her to break silence? Some ministers will permit the returned missionary to stand in the pulpit at home and declare the wonders of His grace, yet deny the women of his congregation any public voice. Is a woman missionary violating the admonition to absolute silence in the church any less than the woman evangelist?

Dr. W.H. Savage of First Baptist Church of Pontiac, Michigan once said concerning the church: "Imagine three women meeting together in the name of the Lord Jesus Christ, longing to worship Him in song and testimony, but all three speechless, because a woman's voice must not be heard glorifying God!" And then he adds, "Let's be consistent; either a woman's voice must not break the silence of any assembly, whether small or large; or, give her an opportunity, if the Spirit so leads, to proclaim the gospel."[19]

"O consistency, thou art a jewel!"

Chapter Eleven

GLIMPSES INTO CHURCH HISTORY

N ow that we have viewed leading women of biblical history and considered some of the key Bible teachings on the role of women, let us consider some ministering women of the succeeding years of church history. As early as the first century women played a considerable part in Christian ministry, especially in the areas of teaching and missionary work. So revolutionary was the power of the Gospel in early church times that Libanius, the heathen philosopher, exclaimed, "What women these Christians have!"[1]

Even in the dark ages of the fourth century, according to Dwight M. Pratt, women's activity shone brightly:

The type of feminine character produced by Christianity in that era is indicated by such notable examples as . . . Anthusa, Nonna, Monica, respectively the mothers of Chrysostom, Gregory . . . and Augustine. Like the mothers of Jerome and Ambrose, they gave luster to the womanhood of the early Christian centuries by their accomplishments and eminent piety. As defenders of the faith, women stand side by side with Ignatius and Polycarp in their capacity to face death and endure the

agonies of persecution. The role of martyrs is made
luminous by Christian maidens as Blondina, . . . Perpe-
tua, and Felicitas, who, in their loyalty to Christ, shrank
not from the most fiendish tortures invented by the
diabolical cruelties and hatred of pagan Rome.[2]

Mr. E.R. Pitman in his book, *Lady Missionaries in Many
Lands*, states:

There is no service in the modern Church upon which
woman has not conferred lustre. Catherine of Sienna
and Elizabeth of Hungary are samples of pre-Reforma-
tion saintly workers; and since the Reformation the list
may be increased a thousandfold. We need only name
Elizabeth Fry, Florence Nightingale, Mary Moffat, and
Sarah Martin, as samples of a whole host of devoted
women who have counted not their lives dear unto
them, so that they could benefit humanity.[3]

Think further of Madame Guyon of France, who by her
deep spiritual teaching made new men of scores of the scholarly but unspiritual Catholic clergy of her time and was
imprisoned for years on account of her *protestant* teaching.
And what about the talented mother of the Wesleys and the
notable Mrs. Fletcher? Prophetesses indeed!

Many people are unaware that great preachers, such as
Charles Finney, John Wesley, and some Puritan reformers
(Congregationalists and Quakers), endorsed the spiritual ministry of women. Dr. A.J. Gordon, the famous missionary
Baptist pastor, also argued strongly for the "ministry of wom-
en" in his book by that title which was published in 1894.
Jonathan Blanchard, the founding president of Wheaton College, declared that "the first alteration which Christianity
made in the polity of Judaism was to abrogate the oppressive
distinction of sexes [in which] woman had almost no rights."[4]

Throughout church history times of spiritual revival have
always been accompanied by the renewed ministry of conse-

crated women who heralded the Good News. And the reverse is historically true: "It seems," says one writer, "as if the decay of women's ministry took place with the decay of Christianity, the rise of the Roman apostasy, and the proud pretensions of an exclusive priesthood."[5]

The pouring out of God's Spirit sweeps away all barriers. Women as well as men manifest the gifts of the Spirit. According to Dr. A.J. Gordon in *The Alliance Weekly*,

> It cannot be denied that in every great spiritual awakening in the history of Protestantism the impulse for Christian women to pray and witness for Christ in the public assembly has been found irrepressible. Observing this fact and observing also the great blessing which has attended the ministry of consecrated women in heralding the Gospel, many thoughtful men have been led to examine the Word of God anew, to learn if it be really so that the Scriptures silence the testimony which the Spirit so signally blesses. To many it has been both a relief and a surprise to discover how little authority there is in the Word for repressing the witness of women in the public assembly, or for forbidding her to herald the Gospel to the unsaved. If this be so, it may be well for the plaintiffs in this case to beware lest, in silencing the voice of consecrated women, they may be resisting the Holy Ghost. The conjunction of these two admonitions of the apostle is significant: "Quench not the Spirit; despise not prophesyings" (1 Thessalonians 5:19, 20)[6]

Mrs. Jessie Penn-Lewis writes,

> So it has been all down through the centuries. . . . The Spirit of God has never been poured forth in any company, in any part of the world, in any nation, without the "handmaids" prophesying, and this as the spontaneous and unvarying result of the Spirit of God moving upon women as well as men, as at Pentecost.[7]

Chapter Twelve

MINISTERING WOMEN IN OUR WESTERN WORLD

Many outstanding women in our Western world have exercised their liberty to speak publicly for the Lord with His manifest blessing. Out of the mouth of some of these worthy witnesses may the truth be confirmed that God is pleased to bless a female ministry. Again we quote: "The Lord giveth the word: the women that publish the tidings are a great host" (Ps. 68:11, RSV).

Corrie Ten Boom (1892–1983)

As the first witness of this great host, we shall consider the Dutch woman Corrie ten Boom. How mightily she has been used of God to preach the Gospel in many countries of the world since her experience in the German concentration camp at Auschwitz during the Second World War! In her book, *Plenty for Everyone*, Corrie tells of her response to certain legalists who objected to her teaching ministry:

I am sometimes asked if I ever encounter the difficulties involved when people show their dislike of women speaking in public; my answer is that I do not experience such problems because I will not go where they do not allow me to speak! On one such occasion, in New Zealand, I received a letter from some people, inviting me to speak in a certain town. They wrote, "You understand that you may not teach us. You can give your testimony, but be scriptural and obey 1 Cor. 14:34, 35."

I replied, "If by this you mean that I must come with a closed Bible, then I cannot accept your invitation. I am always happy to give my testimony to glorify the Lord, but only to underline the Gospel. I come to teach the Word of God, not to talk about my own experiences."

Immediately an answer came, "Forget what we have written. We have heard that God is blessing the meetings where you speak."

Later, after my arrival in that town, we discussed this question.

"But do you not, yourself, have the feeling that you are disobedient?" they questioned me anxiously. "Paul says in both 1 Tim. 2:11-12 and 1 Cor. 14:34-35 that women must be silent."

"Yes, that is so; but we must understand what the words mean and do not mean, and how they apply to this day and age. Peter gave us a picture of the present age in the words of Joel when he quoted, 'I will pour out of my Spirit upon all flesh: and your sons and your daughters shall prophesy.' Now what is prophecy? 1 Cor. says it is [speaking] edification, exhortation, and comfort." . . .

"In 1 Cor. 11:5 we find that women prophesied in the assembly. . . . This verse also says that women prayed in church. Again in Acts 21:9 it is mentioned that Philip's four daughters prophesied, not because prophesying by women was rare, but because it was unusual for four women of one family to do so."

"But 1 Cor. 14:34, 35 clearly states that women must be silent in the church," they insisted.

"I believe this must be interpreted in the light of these other scriptures and should not conflict with them. I am sure that it means that women should be silent when someone else is speaking ('let them ask their own husbands at home'). Miriam, Deborah, Anna: they are all good company for me. We are all given encouragement in Psa. 68:11 where the *Revised Version* says, 'The women that publish the tidings are a great host.' Over and above all this there is one thing to which neither man nor woman dare turn a blind eye: the anointing of the Holy Spirit which alone fits them to speak for God (Acts 2:18)."[1]

Catherine Booth (1829–1890)

Another effective voice that was heard in the past century was that of Catherine Booth, wife of General Booth, who founded The Salvation Army.

Though Catherine [had a conviction from God and] believed strongly in woman's right to speak, she herself [married at 26] was very timid, frail in body and pregnant with three children in the first four and a half years of marriage. . . . She gave her first lecture in 1857 on the subject of temperance and she enjoyed it so much she wrote to her parents: "I only wish I had begun years ago. Had I been fortunate enough to have been brought up amongst the Primitives (Methodists), I believe I should have been preaching now. . . . Indeed I felt quite at home on the platform, far more so than I do in the kitchen."

Gradually she was impelled by God into a more public ministry. . . . In December 1859 she saw a pamphlet by a neighboring minister attacking woman's right to preach. . . . Encouraged by William, Catherine wrote a stinging rebuttal titled *Female Ministry, or Women's Right to Preach the Gospel*.

She noted that women in the early church did pray and prophesy publicly and that this was predicted by the prophet Joel. . . . To prove her point she cited various Greek scholars. . . .

Shortly after she finished her pamphlet, her daughter Emma was born [her fourth child] and during her confinement she was deeply convicted by the Spirit that she should consecrate herself to ministry. "I had no vision, but a revelation to my mind." After a struggle she gave in and vowed to use all her talents for God.[2]

Shortly thereafter her husband, William Booth, was forced through sickness to let Catherine carry on in evangelistic services for two weeks. Later when her husband experienced a complete breakdown in health, Catherine was compelled to supply his place and take charge of his entire evangelistic ministry.

As one biographer notes, "It was she, and not William Booth, who laid the first stone of the Salvation Army." . . . Though Salvation Army letterheads and news stories today declare "William Booth, Founder," the title of her biography is more accurate: *Catherine Booth, the Mother of the Salvation Army*. . . . Before her death in 1890 she had preached to millions.[3]

All those years she was manifestly under the blessed anointing of God.

The Maréchale (1859–1955)

Born to General and Mrs. Booth were four daughters, all of whom became evangelists. "Like Philip the Evangelist of Caesarea, William and Catherine Booth 'had four daughters who did prophesy,' brave and gifted English girls who, [filled] with the Holy Spirit, used their . . . burning eloquence to bring sinners to the mercy-seat."[4]

Eldest of the four daughter-evangelists was Catherine Booth who later became Mrs. Booth-Clibborn, better known as the Maréchale. Early anointed of God as an evangelist, young Catherine began to hold special services at sixteen years of age. She first spoke in public at thirteen, and at that time she yielded to an irresistible inward impulse. Her eldest brother was holding an open-air meeting when this young lassie spoke up with great power, "and she delivered her message with a directness and fluency which compelled attention and proved her a born speaker."[5]

This promising young speaker later became the mother of eight children, yet was able under God to carry on an amazing, far-reaching ministry.

[She] was called to carry the spirit of the Gospel— Christ's own spirit of love—first into many of the cities of England and afterwards, in fulfillment of her distinctive life-work, into France and Switzerland, Holland and Belgium. If her story could be told as it deserves to be, it would stand out as one of the most remarkable modern records of Christian work.[6]

Regarding the effects of her two months of ministry in Brussels, Belgium, she said,

This morning I had a conversation with a senator who is at the head of the party of progress here, and he says that the movement is the most remarkable the city has seen for a hundred years, and that the effects are profound and astonishing. . . . During these two months, [said her biographer], she had daily interviews with men and women crushed under the burden of all kinds of sin—a burden that weighed so heavily on her own spirit that sometimes, instead of delivering an address, she could only fall on her knees and cry to God to forgive all the sins that come from the heart of man— murders, adulteries, thefts, uncleanness, lies, blasphemies—all of which had been confessed to her.[7]

This Spirit-anointed woman faced the denizens of darkness in Paris armed with the panoply of God and with her comrades was not afraid of the gates of hell.

From a recent pamphlet published by The Salvation Army we quote:

> For over a hundred years tens of thousands of women have preached in one capacity or the other in The Salvation Army. Hundreds of thousands of people if not millions have been touched by God through their ministry. As we look at the results we cannot believe that it was or is an evil thing. Beyond any reasonable question God has given many women the gift of public ministry . . . by using it for the salvation of souls all round the world.[8]

Jessie Penn-Lewis (1861–1927)

Another English woman whom God greatly used for many years is Mrs. Jessie Penn-Lewis. While most of her ministry was in England, she also had speaking tours in Sweden, Russia, Finland, Denmark, Canada, and the United States. Many times she spoke at Keswick conferences in England and Scotland. Dr. R.A. Torrey, introducing her at the Moody Training Institute in 1900, described her as "one of the most gifted speakers the world has known."

Some of her struggles and the prejudice she faced are seen in the following comments recorded by her biographer:

> "I saw," *she wrote*, "that God had given me a specific commission to proclaim the message of the Cross, at a time when it had almost ceased to be referred to in the pulpits. I saw also that God miraculously opened doors before me to proclaim this message, which no man could shut, but that the one objection was the fact that I was a

woman. There was no quarrel with the message, there
was no *denial of the Divine seal*, there was no getting away
from the evidence of the results. But none of these
things did away with the fact that I was a woman, and
therefore I could not but see that, whilst God opened
doors for me in some quarters, others were fast closed to
the message I bore, purely and only because I was a
woman. . . .

"I knew only too well what the letter of the Scripture
said, in just three passages of the Apostle Paul's writings, but I was certain in my mind, as I walked with God
and found His will and guidance, and as His message
came to me, that if we only knew the exact original
meaning of those passages, they were bound to be *in
harmony with the working of the Holy Spirit* in the Nine-
teenth Century. I no longer say to the Lord, 'Why hast
Thou made me a woman?' My spirit is now at rest, and I
see why, in spite of all my endeavors by prayer and
action, to retire from the commission which was directly
laid upon me, I was not able to get free, for *God had a
deeper intention* in making me a woman, and giving me
the marked approval and guidance of His Spirit in the
service He had called me to.⁹"

Not only did Mrs. Penn-Lewis minister in speaking but also
in her writings. She founded *The Overcomer*, a magazine for
Christian workers, and wrote several books and dozens of
small pamphlets, many of which are still in print. Christians
the world over have been signally challenged and led into a
life of victory through her penetrating messages on the Cross
in the life of the believer.

Henrietta Mears (1890–1963)

Coming closer to home, we think of Henrietta Mears, affectionately known as "Teacher" by thousands of students in
her classes at Hollywood Presbyterian Church. She was led of

God to instruct and inspire many outstanding leaders, such as Bill Bright, founder of Campus Crusade, and Richard Halverson, for many years a leading pastor in Washington, D.C. and chaplain of the United States Senate. Her biographer writes,

> To challenge young men to enter the ministry was perhaps the greatest of Miss Mears' gifts. In the course of her career in Hollywood, over four hundred collegians heard God's call and turned their energies to pulpits in America or to missionary stations scattered around the world.[10]

Dr. Mears had 567 officers and teachers in her huge Sunday School, in which she herself taught the college class. In addition, she founded Gospel Light Publications. In commendation of her work Dr. Harold John Ockenga once wrote to Dr. Mears the following tribute:

> What a work you have done! There is no young peoples' . . . work in this nation equal to yours. When I think of the tens of thousands of people who have studied the Bible under your leadership, of the thousands of young people who have faced the claims of Christ and made a commitment to Him, of the hundreds of young men who have gone into the ministry, and other young people into Christian service, I cannot but stand back in amazement. . . . It was one of my fondest hopes to have you as a professor of Christian Education at Fuller Theological Seminary. Your contribution to ministers would have been the acme of your educational career.[11]

Emma Dryer

Dwight L. Moody referred to Emma Dryer as "one of the best teachers of the Word of God in the United States."[12]

More than any other individual she worked with Moody to establish the training school in Chicago that later became Moody Bible Institute.

In her early years Emma served as principal of Illinois State Normal University. At the time of the great Chicago fire in 1871, she was appointed superintendent of the YWCA, which D.L. Moody had recently helped to establish. "For two years she labored with other volunteers to help the families of Chicago put their lives back together."[13]

After this emergency she planned to return to the university to continue her teaching, but Moody told her, "That is good work for its kind, but there are teachers enough, who want to teach school, and schools enough that want them; but there aren't enough to do this work, and this is the best work."[14] Emma laid the matter before the Lord and in 1873 left public school teaching in order to start training centers for Christian workers in Chicago.

Later Dr. Charles A. Blanchard, president of Wheaton College and pastor of Moody Church, encouraged her to organize special Bible classes, which she patterned after the Mildmay Institutes in England. These "May Institutes" grew year by year until Miss Dryer was convinced that a permanent training school must be started in Chicago. In February of 1887, after raising $250,000, she called the business meeting where the constitution was adopted for the newly formed Chicago Evangelization Society—later to be known as Moody Bible Institute. In a recent *Moody Monthly* article Eric Fellman states that without her "unfailing faithfulness and tremendous educational and organizing abilities, Moody Bible Institute would not exist today."[15]

Maxine Hancock

Still another woman's voice being widely used today in effective public speaking is that of Mrs. Maxine Hancock of Marwayne, Alberta, whose ministry has been highly acceptable from the platform of Prairie Bible Institute. Apparently her early fellowship of believers must have made it difficult for her to realize her Christian liberty to exercise her gift as a public speaker.

In response to our request she sent us this special word of personal testimony.

Several years ago, frustrated by lack of opportunity within a small local fellowship, I shared with a friend my concern that my gifts were lying dormant. "Don't forget what the Word says," she comforted me, " 'A man's gifts maketh room for himself and bringeth him before great men.' God who gave the gifts will open the way for their use." My friend's words have proven prophetic.

Through limiting and even thwarting circumstances, the gifts of teaching and exhorting given to me were channelled into writing, and thus made available to The Body in a wider context that I had ever dreamed. And then, when my first book was published, the opportunities to speak came far faster than I could possibly accept.

I have come to a quiet assurance that when God by His Holy Spirit sees fit to give gifts for public ministry to women, the Church should confidently call forth those gifts. The responsibility lies with The Body to recognize and utilize the Spirit-given gifts of its members. At the same time, the person to whom the gift has been given must await the Lord's timing for the exercise of its ministry.

Finally, I believe that priorities must be maintained. As a wife and mother, I do not consider "public ministry" to be my primary ministry. My primary ministry and use of God's gifts is within my home, serving my family. Writing is secondary to that "private ministry," and speaking is a spin-off from writing. I find that when these priorities are maintained, everything can be done "decently and in order" under the control and direction of the Holy Spirit—and all for the glory of the Lord Jesus Christ.[16]

Dorothy Ruth Miller (1873–1944)

From 1928 to 1943 we were privileged to have Miss Dorothy Ruth Miller on the faculty at Prairie Bible Institute. In her college years she had specialized in English at Columbia University and in history at New York University. Recognizing her gift of teaching, Miss Miller's pastor encouraged her to attend Bible school. During her second term at Nyack Bible College in New York she was asked to teach there. At a later date Dr. Blanchard, then president of Wheaton College, offered her the chair of Bible at Wheaton; but she declined the offer, feeling this position was a man's place.

By the time she came to Prairie, however, Miss Miller had taught many young men and women in various educational circles and had written that notable work, *Ancient History in Bible Light*. At one time she received an inquiry from an Alberta Baptist pastor's wife regarding whether preaching occasionally for her husband was scriptural. Here is part of Miss Miller's reply:

> In the first place let me say that as a girl I never took kindly to the idea of women preachers or doctors. So far as I can remember this arose from a rather poor opinion of women's intellects. Rather funny, is it not?
>
> Then after the Lord saved me I had no idea of being a Bible teacher. In the Sunday School of the Baptist church of which I was a member, there was an adult's class of which both men and women were members. I was chosen teacher of this class. The pastor of the church, a man strongly tinged with Plymouth Brethren teaching, used sometimes to sit in this class and listen. One day after class, he said, "Miss Ruth, you have an unusual gift of teaching the Bible. Such a gift is from the Lord. You ought to go to Bible school and prepare to be a Bible teacher." His words smote me to the heart. I did not have such an ambition. I was teaching school and expected to continue in that work. But I could not escape those words. After about two years I went to

Bible school. I had not been in the school three months when I was asked to take a class. The second year I was asked to teach two classes. Before my graduation I was asked to remain as a regular member of the teaching staff. Those who voiced this call were all men.

I tell you all this because up to this point I had been led at each step not so much by the teaching of Scripture as by the still small voice of the Spirit. All through my Christian service I have had the clear, definite witness of the Spirit (I do not mean a sound of a voice) that I was in His will as to my service. This had been such a real thing to me that I can never understand people's saying that they could not understand how to get the guidance of God. It seems to me that it would be difficult to avoid knowing it. . . .

Now, as to 1 Cor. 14. As you know, the subject of the chapter from first to last is tongues. The matter of women's speaking is brought in in connection with disorderly meetings in which both men and women were speaking in tongues. I suppose that the women added greatly to the disorder and Paul insisted upon their silence.

To me it seems quite certain that these Christian women were making their Christian liberty an excuse for doing in public what no heathen woman could have done and been considered respectable. In that day only courtesans [prostitutes] took part in any prominent way in public gatherings.

The salient point here is the "being in obedience." . . . The law does not say, "keep silence", it says "be in obedience." I fear that this is not always observed by those women who are strong on silence in the churches. They do not learn of their husbands at home but lay down the law to them.

Now, if we accept from our hearts this decree of God vesting headship in the man, then other things fall into order. There will be no "usurping of authority," no "teaching" in the way of laying down the law to a man. . . .

We know that there were women in the early Church who prophesied (Acts 21:9). It seems evident that Paul did not forbid them to prophesy (1 Cor. 11:5). . . . That the "silence" is a matter of yieldedness is shown by 1 Tim. 2:12. It is "all subjection."

If your husband thinks you should not bring the message when he is away, then as a Christian wife, you should not do it. If the elders of your church object to your doing so, then you should keep silence gladly. But if they feel that you have a gift that God can use as a blessing in their church, then, I should say have one of them lead the service and you give the message. Let a man be very evidently at the head. Let it be evident that you are in subjection and that the very fact of your giving the message springs from your subjection to man's headship. This is the way God has led me.[17]

Amy Lee Stockton

As a preschooler Amy Lee Stockton was led to Christ by her Sunday School teacher, and at the early age of five she heard God's voice saying, "I claim your life. I want you in my service. You are mine." Miss Stockton tells of the battle that followed and the subsequent victory:

Immediately there was rebellion—rebellion that persisted through childhood and early youth. . . .

"No, Jesus" was my answer, "ten thousand times, No! There are others—men, young men, strong men. Surely you cannot need me—a little girl of five." Never for one moment, however, of one day that followed, was I unmindful of that moment when God said, with all the persuasion, power, and finality of God: "You belong to Me!"

There came another day, however, in that same

sunny California when my rebellion ceased. Upon my knees by the side of my bed, a struggle was entered into which forever ended all struggles—my Lord had won! . . .

As I arose from my knees, my soul was gripped with an unwavering conviction and my heart was filled with a deep and consuming peace. God's call had been answered. God's will was mine. That conviction the opposing powers of the universe could not shake, nor that peace could they disturb. . . .

Tell me not that I followed the inclination of my own heart. You have my sincere testimony that all the powers of my being were arrayed against the Lord and His desire regarding my life. To preach the Gospel meant for me the facing of an opposition so bitter and unrelenting that because of it my heart was all but broken. It meant for me the sacrifice of much that the world counts great.

From a selfish, worldly standpoint, by responding to His call, I had nothing to gain but everything to lose. God knows my heart when I declare that to enter Christian service I had not the slightest desire. As for preaching—I had never given that vocation a thought. Had it been considered, it would have been desired least of all. Logically it must be conceded [that] the service of Christ I did not enter because of selfish ambition or desire, or any inclination of my own heart.

. . . My bitterest opponent would never think of accusing Satan of thrusting me into the ministry. Of course, one might argue, "Well you know, Satan is clever and subtle. Possibly he deceived you into believing you had received a divine call. He is the arch deceiver! Perhaps you mistook his promptings for God's pleading!"

One's reply to such reasoning is that if Satan is responsible for the service I have rendered through the years, if he planned a ministry blessed with the salvation

of souls . . . [and] if such definite results were the outcome of misdirection through Satanic influences, do you
think that for once Satan overstepped himself? . . .

Through the years of my ministry it has been my
privilege to see great numbers accept my Saviour as their
Saviour and to own my Lord as theirs. They in turn have
led hosts of others to Christ. Many are the ministers in
the pulpits of our nation; many are the missionaries in
the regions beyond who testify they yielded to Christ or
dedicated their lives to service in the campaigns of
evangelism He has enabled me to conduct. . . .

Here, then, is the conclusion of the matter: My task
was undertaken in response to God's call. It was not
self-chosen or Satan-directed. The Lord Himself thrust
me into the sacred and glorious task of preaching His
Word.[18]

As a testimony to Amy Lee Stockton's ministry, the great
Dr. G. Campbell Morgan said,

It has been my privilege and pleasure on several
occasions to be associated with Miss Amy Lee Stockton
. . . in Bible conference work in California. It affords
me the greatest satisfaction to commend [her] unhesitat-
ingly, and without any reservation. . . .

Miss Stockton is fully qualified by theological training and equipped by conspicuous natural ability, and a
devotion which is at once sane and saintly. I do not
hesitate to say that throughout my long experience I
have known no Woman Preacher, in whose ministry I
have found more complete satisfaction.[19]

Chapter Thirteen

WOMEN AND MISSIONS

W omen missionaries by the thousand comprise a great proportion of the foreign missionary forces of the world. Some forty-five years ago William J. Newell quoted the general secretary of a well-known faith missionary society as saying that "they had 20 women volunteers for missionary work, to one man!"[1] More recently one missionary society reports women missionaries in a ratio of two to one over men. Still another missionary secretary tabulates the ratio as three to two.

Women's work in foreign lands has been manifold in its nature and variety. Many women have staffed pioneer stations, doing a man's work because many young men have proved to be disobedient draft dodgers.

In some cultures *only* women can bring the Gospel to pagan women who sit in darkness, for men are not allowed to approach them. The woman missionary, as homemaker and example of God's liberating grace, has the signal opportunity of manifesting to the heathen world what Christ can do for women.

The great missionary movements in the last century, in which both men and women published the Gospel to millions of new hearers, were due largely to three great missionary-

minded men of God: Hudson Taylor, founder of the China
Inland Mission (now the Overseas Missionary Fellowship),
D.L. Moody, evangelist and founder of Moody Bible Insti-
tute, and Frederik Franson, founder of The Scandinavian
Alliance Mission (now The Evangelical Alliance Mission).

Hudson Taylor broke through many barriers of custom,
culture, and prejudice in accepting women as full missionary
members. Before long, however, he was vindicated, because
the thrilling results were indeed convincing. In the biography
of Malla Moe we read that D.L. Moody's encouragement
started her on the course which ended in her serving the Lord
for many years in South Africa. Fredrik Franson also had a
part in her missionary career. Certainly God would not have
led these missionary statesmen to encourage women in Christian work if He Himself did not approve of their service. Can
men honestly face these stubborn facts and at the same time
downgrade the anointing and ministry of chosen women of
God?

Let us look briefly into the lives of some of the great
women missionaries of the past two centuries—women who
have manifestly been in the center of God's will in their
public ministry.

Ann Hasseltine Judson (1789–1826)

In his book *Lady Missionaries in Many Lands* Mr. E.R. Pitman
points out that "the life and memory of Mrs. Ann Judson [of
Burma] are surrounded by an imperishable halo on account of
her being the pioneer of female missionary effort."[2] At the
time she embarked on her missionary career, no woman had
ever left American or European shores to engage in mission
work abroad, though other women followed shortly after.

Concerning her momentous decision to go to India, Ann
Hasseltine wrote as follows:

> Might I but be the means of converting a single soul it
> would be worth spending all my days to accomplish.

. . . At other times I feel ready to sink, and appalled at the prospect of pain and suffering, to which my nature is so averse and apprehensive. But I have at all times felt a disposition to leave it with God, and trust Him to direct me.

I have at length come to the conclusion that if nothing in providence appears to prevent, I must spend my days in a heathen land. I am a creature of God, and He has an undoubted right to do with me as seemeth good in His sight. . . .

Were it not for these considerations, I should with my present prospects sink down in despair, especially as no female has, to my knowledge, ever left the shores of America to spend her life among the heathen.[3]

Amy Carmichael (1867–1951)

Founder and director of Dohnavur Fellowship of India, Amy Carmichael has left an indelible impression upon the entire Christian world through her deeply spiritual writings. Who can question her God-honoring leadership and her lifelong answers to prayer? The Dohnavur Fellowship is a faith mission which still functions with no public appeal for funds. Had Miss Carmichael been out of divine order in founding and leading such a mission, heaven could have denied her appeal for funds. Yet the financial needs of this great mission have been met for years simply in answer to prayer. Her work, so much like that of George Mueller of Bristol and Hudson Taylor of China, is a living testimony to the good pleasure of God with her deeply spiritual leadership.

Pandita Ramabai (1858–1922)

Writing on women's work in India, missionary statesman Dr. Robert Hall Glover refers especially to women's ministry among oppressed wives and mothers. "Absolutely closed to men missionaries, the family life in all its multiform misery can be reached with the healing and purifying touch of Christianity."[4]

Among the many publicly recognized Indian missionaries he cites Pandita Ramabai as "the best known and most worthy of all."

> [She was] universally acknowledged to be the most distinguished woman in India, native or foreign. Her education was so thorough and her intellectual ability so great that the highest title possible for a native woman was conferred upon her. Forsaking idolatry she turned to Christ, and then consecrated herself with a love and devotion truly wonderful to the emancipation of child-wives and child-widows from their terrible bondage. In the famines and pestilences of 1897 and later years her ministry expanded far beyond her original design, as she threw herself into the desperate situation and rescued thousands of girls and women from death, destitution and the base designs of wicked men. Never will the writer forget the privilege he enjoyed of being the guest of this remarkable woman in her great Christian settlement known as *"Mukti"* [salvation], and addressing her "family" of many hundred sweet-faced little child-widows. Her schools, orphanage and rescue home have witnessed some wonderful outpourings of the Holy Spirit and the conversion of great numbers of souls.[5]

Louisa Vaughan

While at Bible School in Kansas City, we were privileged to meet and hear Louisa Vaughan, who had been a fruitful missionary in China from 1896 to 1912. Listening to her, we almost felt that "never man spake like this" woman.

On one occasion she arrived for a four-day conference of Christians at Yuen Dswang. The Chinese pastor who had invited her concluded their first interview by slamming the door behind him as he walked away, muttering "That's what

I get for asking a woman anything! What does she know?"

That evening this pastor was about to give out the text of his address when the Holy Spirit prompted Miss Vaughan to rise and ask, "Won't you give us five minutes for personal prayer? And let each one pray, 'Heavenly Father, forgive me my sins, send the Holy Spirit into my heart and reveal them to me. Cleanse me from them in the precious blood and fill me with Thy Spirit.' "

Rather reluctantly, the incensed minister, Ding Le Mei, consented, repeated her request, and added "Let us kneel and offer this prayer together."

The Holy Spirit came upon the assembly so suddenly and with such mighty power, that before their knees touched the floor, they were all, as with one voice, sobbing aloud their sins of omission and commission, sins of neglect of the spiritual lives of their children, of not loving one another and not loving God, sins of quarreling, of covetousness, of hatred, and of Sabbath breaking.[6]

A long period of weeping, confession, and restitution followed, with Pastor Ding begging Miss Vaughan to forgive him for his rudeness.

After the conference ended Chinese Christians and leaders who had come to us from a distance returned home. . . . Everywhere they proclaimed the news of our great answers to prayer and requests for similar meetings began to pour in. Pastor Ding and I responded as fully as our physical strength permitted. For seven months we went from conference to conference. . . . At every conference the Spirit was poured out in power and blessing.

Pastor Ding Le Mei had entered upon his life's work as an evangelist. . . . It was arranged for him to visit all the schools, colleges, and universities throughout China. God has so marvellously empowered him that he is known today as the "Apostle of China" and "China's Moody."[7]

And he was led to such a Spirit-anointed ministry through the agency of a mere woman!

Mildred Cable and Francesca French

In the Far East two missionary heroines, Mildred Cable and Francesca French, labored many years in rugged pioneer work with the China Inland Mission. They preached the Gospel in western China and central Asia with great blessing, and have written a number of books on various aspects of their outstanding career.

Irene Webster-Smith (Sensei) (1888–1971)

Climaxing many years of missionary service, Irene Webster-Smith founded a great work for Christ in Japan after she was threescore years of age.

> With only $18 to her name she bought a house in Tokyo to establish a Christian Student Centre. And despite the fact that its price was $18,000, she never once missed a payment. Fourteen years later the property was worth $1,000,000.
>
> [She was used in the conversion] of fourteen of the toughest war criminals in Japan shortly before their execution. When refused permission to visit Nishizawa San, one of the doomed men, she marched calmly into General MacArthur's office with her demand. Not only did he grant it—he had her driven in state to the jail in an army staff car.[8]

Gladys Aylward (1902–1970)

God used Miss Gladys Aylward, better known as "the Small

Woman," in the preaching of the Gospel in China and For-
mosa. "God led her by incredible ways to a ministry among
Chinese men, from rough, pack-mule drivers to military officers and even mandarins.[9]

So self-effacing was this Small Woman that to her these
great exploits in China were nothing remarkable. In fact her
biographer, Alan Burgess, could scarcely elicit from her the
exciting details. According to him,

> She is one of the most remarkable women of our
> generation. . . . She possesses that inner exaltation,
> that determination to go on, unto death, which adversi-
> ty, torture, brain-washing and hardship cannot eradicate
> from the human soul, and which is the natural corollary
> of a tenacity of faith so unusual in an age of little faith.[10]

Mary Taft

"Mrs. Mary Taft, the talented wife of the Rev. Dr. Taft, was
another eminently successful labourer in the Lord's [African]
vineyard." A fellow-worker commented,

> An eminent minister informed us that of those who had
> been brought to Christ through her labours, over two
> hundred entered the ministry. She seldom opened her
> mouth in public assembly, either in prayer or speaking,
> but the Holy Spirit accompanied her words in such a
> wonderful manner, that sinners were convicted, and, as
> in apostolic times, were constrained to cry out, "What
> must we do to be saved?"[11]

Mary Slessor (1848–1915)

Over a half century ago Dr. Robert H. Glover painted this
thumbnail sketch of Mary Slessor of Calabar:

> Her life-story rivals in many particulars that of David

Livingstone. She served in Africa under the *United Free Church of Scotland* from 1876 to 1915. From an unlettered factory girl in the homeland she advanced into the foremost rank of missionary pathfinders. Her work was that of a pioneer among the most savage tribes of the Calabar hinterland. Practically single-handed she tamed and transformed three pagan communities in succession. It is a question if the career of any other woman missionary had been marked by so many strange adventures, daring feats, signal providences, and wonderful achievements.[12]

Here is one brief paragraph from Mary Slessor's own pen:

My life is one long daily, hourly record of answered prayer, for physical health, for [relief from] mental overstrain, for guidance given marvellously, for errors and dangers averted, for enmity to the Gospel subdued, for food provided at the exact hour needed, for everything that goes to make up life and my poor service. I can testify, with a full and often wonder-stricken awe, that I believe that God answers prayer.[13]

Malla Moe

Another outstanding missionary was Malla Moe, one of the longest-serving and most fruitful missionaries to South Africa. Her ministry was to both men and women, and she won thousands to the Lord.

As a young woman of twenty-three she heard evangelist D.L. Moody preach. At the close of his sermon he said, "All Christians get to work, and all sinners come forward." Although she was already saved, she stayed to hear more preaching from Moody, hoping that she would not be noticed. Moody spotted her, however, and after discovering she was a Christian, challenged her with the question, "If you are saved, then why don't you go to work?"[14]

Shortly after, she attended meetings conducted by

Frederik Franson, who was recruiting missionary volunteers to open work in Africa, and told Malla, "God wants you to be a missionary to Africa."[15] And to Africa she went.

Joy Ridderhof (1903–1984)

During the fall and winter of 1937 Miss Joy Ridderhof was at home in Los Angeles, seeking to recover from a severe illness so that she could return to her mission field in Honduras. Her health did not improve sufficiently for this, but God gave her a vision for reaching the otherwise unreached by means of gramophone records. And Gospel Recordings was born.

Under God's blessing the little mission rapidly expanded so that by 1960 over 2 million records in over 2,000 different languages had been sent out. Phyllis Thompson tells of the remarkable growth of this work in her book, *Faith by Hearing*, published by Gospel Recordings. A few years later Joy Ridderhof herself gave the same exciting account in Prairie Tabernacle. Today most countries of the earth are hearing the Gospel message from these simple gramophone records.

Helen Roseveare

Dr. Helen Roseveare, medical doctor, gifted author and speaker, served many years in Zaire with Worldwide Evangelistic Crusade. Many times at Prairie Bible Institute she has captivated our large conference crowds with her accounts of missionary pioneering, fruitful suffering, and wonderful achievement in Zaire. Dr. Roseveare was God's leading voice, we understand, at the 1978 Student Missionary Conference at Urbana, Illinois. Today she is being used by WEC International in a full-time speaking ministry in Bible conferences, Bible colleges, universities (under Inter-Varsity Christian Fellowship sponsorship), and women's conferences throughout the English-speaking world.

Chapter Fourteen

PERSISTENT PREJUDICE

In spite of the liberating power of the Gospel, strong prejudice against woman's public ministry has persisted in certain segments of the church throughout its history. Some of God's choicest servants—missionaries, teachers, and evangelists—have been sorely hindered, severely criticized, and needlessly stymied. Their intolerable fault? They were *women*. We might assemble a whole galaxy of women who have been lightbearers of the Gospel message in the face of such opposition, but let us notice a few who are typical of the many.

Dr. A.J. Gordon relates the following incident:

We vividly remember, in the early days of women's work in the foreign field, how that brilliant missionary to China, Miss Adele Fielde, was recalled by her Board because of the repeated complaints of the senior missionaries that in her work she was transcending her sphere as a woman. "It is reported that you have taken upon you to preach," was the charge read by the chairman: "Is it so?" She replied by describing the vastness and destitution of her field—village after village, hamlet after hamlet yet unreached by the Gospel—and then

how, with a native woman, she had gone into the surrounding country, gathered groups of men, women, and
children—whoever would come—and told out the story
of the cross to them. "If this is preaching, I plead guilty
to the charge," she said. "And have you ever been
ordained to preach?" asked her examiner. "No," she
replied, with great dignity and emphasis—"no; *but I
believe I have been foreordained.*"[1]

Catherine Booth preached to millions during her lifetime.
When a legalistic minister published a pamphlet attacking
woman's right to preach, Catherine Booth wrote a stinging
rebuttal, citing such biblical examples as Deborah, Huldah,
Miriam, and Anna. She concluded with the following
paragraph:

If the Word of God forbids female ministry, we would
ask how it happens that so many of the devoted handmaidens of the Lord have felt themselves constrained by
the Holy Ghost to exercise it? Surely there must be
some mistake somewhere, for the Word and Spirit cannot contradict each other. Either the Word does not
condemn women preaching, or these confessedly holy
women have been deceived.[2]

Mrs. Booth was one of the first to assert woman's liberty
as a public speaker, and her daughters entered into her sacred
heritage. Most noteworthy is Mrs. Booth-Clibborn, better
known as the Maréchale, whose life work as an evangelist
issued in the salvation of many thousands in France, Switzerland, and Belgium. She could never entertain any secret
bondage of fear that her ministry could be grieving the Spirit
of God even though she met with strong opposition as a
woman preacher. "It was impossible," says her biographer,
"that she should work for years without encountering many
who had strong prejudices. Our Lord's disciples 'marvelled
that He spoke with a woman,' and there are still disciples

who marvel when a woman speaks for Him."³

The Maréchale's methods naturally gave offense to those who had not the courage to adopt them. Late one night she and some comrades were standing at the door of a theatre while it was emptying. One of her young officers cried in clear, penetrating tones, "Prepare to meet thy God!" The words seemed to send an electric shock through the gay crowd. Thereupon a gentleman came forward to the Maréchale and said:

"Mademoiselle, you are evidently young girls of good family, and I am scandalised [*sic*] to see you here at this hour. I, too, occupy myself with preaching, but I am shocked at your behaviour."

"Really?" she replied, "and I am scandalised that you are scandalised. You profess to believe the Gospel. How are to you get these indifferent tens of thousands to hear of the Saviour? They won't come to listen to you. What more natural and more in accord with the principles of Jesus, than to go to them and compel them to hear?"

Ten minutes after, the gentleman returned and slid a five-franc piece into her hand, saying:

"It is you who are right!"⁴

M. Lassaire, a great Catholic scholar whose translation of the four Gospels was honored by his church, came to the Maréchale before the latter's departure from France and said, "You ought not to leave us. God has given you the ear of the nation as it is given only once in a hundred years."⁵ An eminent statesman in Brussels was so moved by her spiritual ministry that he said, "Everybody has been ridiculed here except you. Ridicule kills everything; you have killed ridicule."⁶ Is there any wonder that old General Booth said, "Our best men are women"?

In the 1930s Mr. and Mrs. Raymond Frame of the Overseas Missionary Fellowship were serving in the Bible Institute of the Philippines. At one time Mr. Frame was troubled by the Scripture that he should be committing these things "to faithful *men*" (2 Tim. 2:2, italics his). He says,

> At first my heart sank a bit—"So . . . I ought to be training men." Then I checked a Greek New Testament to see what word St. Paul had used for "men" in this verse. I must admit that I was quite relieved to discover that Paul's language meant, "commit to faithful persons" and not necessarily, "commit to faithful males. . . . Already a number of our lady graduates, equally with the men, are busy committing to other faithful persons the eternal truths that we have worked so hard to make clear and real to them."[7]

In 1957 Ingrid Stippa completed her studies at Prairie Bible Institute. Three years later she sailed on the *Queen Mary* for Borneo. Before she boarded the ship, the head of her mission suggested she go to the purser and offer to take the Protestant service being held in the large lounge area of the ship. Although a shy 29-year-old first-term missionary, she offered and the offer was accepted. She picked out the hymns and planned the order of service, which she conducted for 100 people including 30 returning missionaries. Many were blessed, and some came up to shake her hand and to ask where she was going. One of the male missionaries pressed a tract into her hand and asked her to read it back in her stateroom. The substance of the tract was, "It is a sin for women to preach!"[8] And perhaps that missionary would have been the last to witness in the way Miss Stippa had done. Shame on that legalist!

Leatha Humes, one of Prairie's early high school teachers went to Indonesia as a missionary. There her main ministry was the preparation of a Bible curriculum for use in all public schools. During a recent furlough she attended Gordon-Conwell Theological Seminary to earn her master's degree in Christian Education and was later awarded an honorary doctorate. Here is her own story of an encounter she had with some college students when she was on furlough in the United States:

> After I told of helping in a workshop for 300 Religious Instruction teachers for grade school (all men), a group of college students cornered me and wanted me to explain how I could teach men in view of what Paul had said. I'm sure the Lord gave the answer, for the question came unexpectedly and had to be answered on the spot. I told them I was not "running that show" and it had not been my idea to go there to teach, but I had been sent there by the man who is my boss and I had been put on the program by the men who were in charge of the workshop. So I passed the question back to them. "Do you think I should have refused to do what my boss asked me to do when I was the only one available with the training needed to do that job? Would that not have been insubmission?" They seemed quite content with the answer and I was thankful.

Some years ago a devoted woman founded a successful foreign missionary work which thrived as long as she was the director. During her ministry she led many to Christ and influenced a number of young men and women to give their lives for Christian service. One such young man is today an outstanding evangelist and radio preacher in his home country. He tells that he not only found Christ but began his training in Christian service under that English *woman* missionary!

After the founder's death, her obvious successor was her coworker—another woman. But certain legalistic men from our fundamental world insisted upon *male* leadership. Facing what seemed an impossible situation, this coworker finally had to withdraw. The national pastors, recognizing in her the God-ordained leader of the work, *withdrew with her*. The net result of this insistence? The work died. Yes indeed, "the letter killeth."

Another noble missionary, Mrs. Grattan Guinness, shows why women so often have to assume the leadership:

When so many ministers of the stronger and wiser sex are useless or worse than useless in the work of soul saving, and preach for years without being instrumental in a single conversion, *is there not a cause* for woman's ministry? . . . Had Barak better played the man, Deborah had better played the woman.

. . . Had the disciples tarried longer at the sepulchre, Mary need not have been the first proclaimer of the resurrection of our Lord. Had Balaam been a more faithful prophet, the ass need never have opened *her* mouth.[9]

Here is a voice from the Open Brethren, G.H. Lang:

I feel quite unable to require, in effect, that men must perish eternally rather than that a woman should tell them the good tidings. Let any good brother who feels strongly in the other direction that a woman must be utterly silent in the public presence of men consider whether, if *he* were unconverted, he would prefer to go to hell rather than be saved through a woman preaching?

For myself, having been called by God to see with my own eyes and feel with my own soul the unutterable need of the millions of mankind yet in Satanic darkness, I can but thank God from the depths of my heart for everyone, man or woman, that takes to them the Word of life.[10]

My prayer is that God will use the above witnesses to help many a young woman to take her rightful place of service, privilege, and honor as one of the King's daughters. How sad that the prevailing prejudice against women's participation in public ministry deters some from heeding God's call to service!

Men's Chauvinism

In commenting on the sex question it seems that most theologians of the past, being chiefly men, were overly occupied with what a woman should *not* do. While claiming male monopoly of privilege and position, they failed to stir up their own sex to a fervent evangelistic and missionary spirit.

Of course man as constituted with his aggressive leadership is fitted to head and to administer and to carry responsibility, but from humanity's earliest days man has perverted his position and asserted his lordship. He has considered himself the master and has looked upon woman as merely "a helpmeet for man—not his correspondent or *counterpart*, but his subordinate and servant, or at best his [inferior] helper—that is, man, the superior and sovereign; woman, the subject and servant."[11]

God's plan, however, is that men and women should complement each other in all areas of life, including Christian service.

> The law of sex runs through all Christian work. The feminine element is needed as well as the masculine. Man may be aggressive, bold, strong, fitted to pioneer, organize, administer; but woman is patient, impressive, tender, sympathetic, fitted to win, to soothe, to comfort, to minister. Both together bring to the work the complete furnishing that leaves no element of adaptation lacking.[12]

To our legalistic way of thinking we might question God's having broken His own rule in His occasional choice of female instruments to occupy the public position to which He manifestly called them. We must acknowledge, though, that certain women have been singled out for special public ministry, persons who in the natural seem most unqualified to occupy the position to which God calls them. Yet thereby are they all the better qualified for bringing praise and honor to the all-wise Head of the church, for "God hath chosen the foolish things of the world to confound the wise; and God hath chosen the weak things of the world to confound the things which are mighty . . . that no flesh should glory in His presence" (1 Cor. 1:27-29).

The Rev. J.P. Millar in his *Homiletic Commentary on the Book of Judges*, says concerning God's choice of Deborah and Jael,

> Who could have supposed that two women would have been put in the foreground to meet this most serious juncture in Israel's history—the one to act as the head, and the other as the hand, in vanquishing and even in annihilating the formidable power that had ground Israel to the dust for twenty years! Had a Joshua been raised up to act as leader, then glory might have been ascribed to the great captain that led Israel's armies. But when a Deborah and a Jael are employed to do the work, then is it all the more conspicuous, that the hand of the Lord had brought about the result.[13]

Exceptions to the Rule?

Would some say when God chooses to use a woman in public service, He always does so as an exception to the rule, and only does so when there are no men prepared for the task? While it is true that at times God may choose a woman to perform an outstanding public service because no suitable man is at hand, yet it is also evident in Scripture as well as in later history that a woman is sometimes chosen above a qualified and available man.

Occasionally it has been my glad privilege to minister the Word of God in a Brethren Assembly. On one such occasion we "remembered the Lord" in the morning service. Then we had a much blessed afternoon service, at the close of which we did the unorthodox thing (according to that Assembly) of giving an altar call for consecration. The front of the Assembly was filled with believers seeking a deeper experience with the Lord. At the evening service the leading elder exhorted the believers in a strong appeal: "Now, friends, we are getting our graveclothes off; if only we could get our mouths open." This good brother, a worthy church elder, was deeply concerned over the manifest bondage of the members of that Assembly, both men and women. He was convinced that out from the innermost being of all believers there should flow rivers of living water. He felt that both men and women needed not only to get their graveclothes off but to get their mouths open in public praise and testimony.

For his having taken the liberty to have this writer speak to his Assembly, this elder was later taken to task by the nearby assembly of "Closed Brethren." Their registered reproof of him was, "At the Prairie Bible Institute *women* as well as men are allowed to speak in public assemblies!"

Our brother answered his critics very well: "We, brethren, have our returning foreign missionaries, women as well as men, address our assemblies."

Their stock reply was, "That is different; that is an exception."

"Not a bit of it," our brother rightly retorted.

Where is the Assembly at home or abroad that is so sacrosanct that no feminine voice may be heard? Consider the foreign mission field, even among Christian Brethren missions. One of the happier signs of the times is that the Plymouth Brethren have sent single women abroad as missionaries to spread the glad tidings where they must teach men as well as women who have been converted through their preaching. Such women come home and, contrary to their church's rule which silences women, publicly report to their waiting assemblies on the progress of the Gospel. We can but ask, "Are these women disobeying the Spirit of God in their public ministry?"

In his commentary on the Book of Romans, Dr. William

R. Newell relates the following:

> There was a wonderful old saint in St. Louis, Mother Gray, humble, teachable, earnest, and mightily filled with the Holy Spirit. When she rose, with her back bowed with many, many years of physical and spiritual labour, and her reverent head covered with her little black bonnet, and began to testify, to exhort, or to pray, everyone was moved, and even the Plymouth Brethren (my best helpers not only in St. Louis, but generally, whenever it has been my privilege to preach), said to me, "Mother Gray seems an exception."
>
> No, she was not an exception, any more than was dear old "Auntie Cook," in Chicago, who with another sister prayed unceasingly for D.L. Moody till he was mightily anointed with the Spirit of God.
>
> And there was "Holy Ann" in Toronto, her little, feeble frame bent with years, but filled with the Spirit of God. Standing up to testify in the great Cooke's Church one afternoon, being very short, she gave her hand to be lifted, and stood on the pew! And we shall never forget her exhortation, *for God was in it!*[14]

At Holy Ann's funeral in Toronto there were ministers from all denominations gathered around the casket. The large city church was packed to the doors. Hundreds listened to the testimony of those representing all branches of the Christian church. This would not have seemed strange had the coffin contained the remains of one of earth's great ones, but this woman was poor and illiterate, with her very coffin a gift of love and her dust deposited in the lot of another. On the following Sunday the Mayor of Toronto testified in his church,

> I had two honours this week. It has been my privilege to have an interview with the President of the United States. This is a great honour. Then I have been pall-

bearer to Holy Ann. Of the two honours I prize the latter most.[15]

Would some biased brethren consider such women as Mother Gray, Auntie Cook, Holy Ann and a host of others to be exceptions to the rule? We grant that they were exceptional in their faith and fearless utterance, but obviously their audible service in the presence of both men and women should not be regarded as an exception to the rule (unless it be the rule and regulation of man). Rather, their godly ministry tests the rule and proves that the total embargo on woman's audible ministry is legalistic and that "the letter killeth, but the Spirit giveth life" (2 Cor. 3:6).

We could enumerate many other female witnesses who have functioned in a most outstanding way for the Lord, but we forbear. With so many *exceptions*, however, some of us should begin to examine what we have regarded as an unbreakable rule for the role of women in public service. It seems to us that these many exceptions serve to disprove the legalistic rule that would silence all women. Surely these many examples constitute adequate testimony to free other Christian women from needless bondage and give them confidence to go forward, if God leads, to exercise their liberty in audible public ministry.

Only where the Gospel of Christ has penetrated do we find that women have true liberty and freedom. Go to China, to India, to Africa, and other places where Christianity is not known; and you will see women enslaved, oppressed, and degraded. But where the Gospel is preached, where the love of Jesus is magnified, and where the victory of Calvary is proclaimed, there woman is given her proper place as revealed in the Word of God.

Chapter Fifteen

GOD'S PATTERN FOR THE HOME

I n Ephesians 5:21-33 the Apostle Paul gives some helpful guidelines for establishing a godly home. Woman's role as set forth in this passage is to submit to her husband as the head of the home. If the husband fulfills his God-given role and responsibility, the wife will have nothing to fear; she will find sufficient motivation in the phrase "as unto the Lord" (v. 22). When by grace her subjection is made gladly, corresponding joy is sure to follow.

Note the lofty pattern the Lord gives to illustrate this relationship: "For the husband is the head of the wife, even as Christ is the head of the church" (v. 23). Therefore, "as the church is subject to Christ, so let the wives also be to their own husbands in everything" (v. 24). So the Word of God declares that the headship of man is to reflect the headship of the Man Christ Jesus over His beloved bride, the church.

What a privilege is given to the woman—to exemplify and express a purpose and relationship so divinely marvelous! To you, beloved woman in Christ, is the high honor given of demonstrating to angels, as well as to all on earth, the blessed union of Christ and His blood-bought church.

The Husband's Headship

The headship of the husband is of divine ordering for the home. Such a headship shadows forth the relationship between God and Christ. In our chapter 8 we noticed that "the head of every man is Christ; and the head of the woman is the man; and the head of Christ is God" (1 Cor. 11:3). The submission of Christ as Son to the Father does not mean that the Son is inferior to the Father, nor does it cast any doubt upon Christ's deity. Likewise the wife's subjecting herself to her husband does not mean that she is inferior or that as image-bearer she is not equal with her husband. Just as no inferiority may be attributed to Christ in His voluntary subjection to God, so also no inferiority may be assumed for the Christian wife in her voluntary subjection to her husband. Let us forever put aside any thought of superiority on the husband's part or of inferiority on the wife's part. The passage carries no thought of slavish obedience to every whim and fancy of an unreasonable selfishness on the part of the husband but rather implies loyal subjection in love.

Such a joyous and voluntary subjection on the woman's part will seldom, if ever, need the command, "Let the wife see to it that she respect her husband" (v. 33, NASB). She would be a strange wife indeed who would not respect a husband who loves her as Christ loves His church! (v. 25)

One of the sad and serious signs of our day is the lordly domineering of many Christian women. Dr. Harry Ironside told of a Christian home where he was given hospitality. It was Sunday morning, and as the folks were hurrying around getting ready for Sunday School, the daughter barked out to the father to hurry up and get ready. Feeling a bit guilty, she turned to Dr. Ironside and remarked, "I hope you'll understand; we have the greatest difficulty getting Daddy to mind." Doubtless this disrespectful daughter had learned her impertinence from an unsubmissive wife and mother. Such overbearing women assume an unscriptural domination that is not of God. Perhaps we should add that the father in that home had likely failed to merit the respect of the household—a respect that a husband cannot command or demand but must win and deserve.

To the husbands Paul says, "Love your wives, even as Christ also loved the church and gave Himself for it" (v. 25). In his position as head of the home the husband is to be to his wife what Christ is in His love relationship to the church (v. 23). The word *head* in v. 23 does not imply a hierarchy but simply suggests the wife's "source" or "origin" as portrayed in Genesis 2:21-23.

Christ's Headship

Now consider briefly in what sense Christ is the Head of His church. Perhaps the fullest explanation is in Colossians 2:19 where He is said to be "the Head, from whom all the body, being supplied and knit together through the joints and bands, increaseth with the increase of God" (ASV). Here we see Christ's headship of support and nourishment and growth. As Head and Bridegroom it is His responsibility to provide all things needful for the well-being of His bride, the church. Through sacrificing His life, Christ won the church as His bride. As He knows our needs, our trials, and our troubles, so He with perfect love and devotion makes full provision to "nourish and cherish" us (Eph. 5:29).

Unfortunately the prevailing concept of headship in the home is not that of provision and care and nourishment, but rather of rule or dominion of the man over the woman. Some would construe headship to mean that man is the master and woman is the servant, but the headship of Christ involved not so much His governmental rule over the church as His care and provision for His church's well-being.

Jesus sets forth an exemplary discipleship like this:

Ye know that the princes of the Gentiles exercise dominion over them, and they that are great exercise authority upon them. But it shall not be so among you: but whosoever will be great among you, let him be your

minister . . . even as the Son of man came not to be
ministered unto, but to minister, and to give His life a
ransom for many. (Matt. 20:25-28)

When Jesus makes an appeal for our complete submission
to Him and to one another, He is not promoting a spirit of
authoritarianism, nor is He denying that some are appointed
to positions of leadership; He simply establishes a precedent
for all Christians—especially for those whose role is that of
leadership or headship. He demonstrates the ideal: how He
Himself came not "to be served, but to serve, and to give His
life a ransom for many" (Mark 10:45, NASB). What a glorious
pattern for harmony between husband and wife!

In a certain meeting where God was working mightily
with men, one husband confessed with tears, "I have been a
brute in my home." We know of a similar case where the
husband was manifestly zealous for God and for the cause of
missions, yet in his own home he was a bully and a tyrant. A
godly Bible teacher once testified of the Lord's dealing about
his relationship with his wife. At that time God's word to him
was, "When you come up to give a personal account before
My throne, I am not going to examine you as to all your
service; I am going to ask you just one thing: How did you
treat your wife?"

In Ephesians 5:21-33 nothing is said about the multiple
faults of either one. Instead, we have a description of the
specific responsibilities of each one, with the stress on love,
honor, and respect. The position of each is plain: the husband is the head; the wife is the suitable helper, completing
him, his other self. This heaven-high standard for each in the
husband-wife relationship, however, is contrary to our fallen
nature—selfless love and consideration.

Now if we consider the wider context of these directions
for the domestic life, we note that the passage opens with the
mutual subjection of *all Christians*—men and women, husbands and wives—yielding to each other under the headship
of the Lord Jesus Christ: "Subjecting yourselves one to

another in the fear of Christ" (v. 21). Here is the strongest
motivation for mutual subjection in all Christian relationships—a godly incentive founded upon the wholesome, rev-
erential fear of displeasing Christ, a purifying dread founded
upon the desire of each to do the whole will of God. This
subjection one to another is not a one-sided subjection, by
which some truly self-deprecating Christian becomes the victim of someone who is lordly, selfish, and domineering, but a
subjection that calls for selflessness and Christlikeness of
each alike.

Harmony in the Home

The Apostle Peter in his first epistle sets forth the divine plan
for harmony in the home. In chapter 2 he makes various
applications of the general idea of subjection or submission
(1 Peter 2:13-20). In 1 Peter 3:1-7 he relates this attitude of
submission to wives and husbands as he deals with the home
life.

Here the admonition to the wives is the same as that laid
down by Paul in Ephesians 5:22-24, Colossians 3:18, and
Titus 2:4-5. Their subjection is to be manifested in their
consistent, godly lives. Christian wives are not to imagine
that their conversion to Christ and their share in all equalities
and Christian privileges exempt them from subjection to their
pagan husbands. Their affectionate submission would be the
most likely way to win a disobedient and unbelieving husband, for most unbelieving husbands would have no other
evidence of Christianity than what they could see in the
humble, prudent, and peaceable behavior of their wives.

Christian wives often fall into reasoning that their husbands can be won only by hearing the Word. But Peter's
concern is that the godly life of the wives so influence the
husbands "that they may without the Word be gained by the
behavior of their wives" (v. 1). "Without the Word" implies
without talking about spiritual things, without torturing them
with truth, hurling texts at them, without asserting equal

rights, and certainly without spiritual lectures, nagging, or haranguing. It seems that some men are so stubborn they will never be won by the Word, but only by the good example of their wives—"even the ornament of a meek and quiet spirit, which is in the sight of God of great price" (v. 4). Simply by being adorned with the radiant beauty of a gentle and quiet spirit are these holy women likely to win their obstinate husbands.

The story is told of a group of Christian women who met regularly to pray for their unsaved husbands. It so happened that one of the husbands objected to his wife's attending these meetings and forbade her to continue. Graciously she submitted to her husband's wishes and, strange as it may seem, was later able to win him to Christ.

In verses 5 and 6 Peter reminds wives of how women of former days exemplified good Christian behavior, "whose children ye now are," if as real Christians you are not "put in fear by any terror" (ASV). The terror here may refer to that fear which could be caused by persecution.

In verse 7 the call comes to husbands: "Likewise, ye husbands, dwell with them according to knowledge, giving honour unto the wife, as unto the weaker vessel." Note the spiritual basis of a harmonious domestic life—"being heirs together of the grace of life"; also, the wonderful result— "that your prayers be not hindered." How beautiful is the completeness of these motives! The husband is to care for the wife because she is weak, and he is to honor her because she is a Christian.

What shall we conclude then to be God's ideal for the home? The husband is to pattern his headship after the pattern of Christ—to support, nourish, and lift up his wife to the level of the great Head of the church. This will mean that he must win a worthy headship, not by exercising some divine right of kingship, but by an unselfish love that lays down its life by a self-sacrificing love, even as our Lord Jesus Christ came to serve and to lay down His own life for the church.

Making It Practical

What will this mean in practice? It will mean that when an argument flares up—and differences and misunderstandings there will be in this life—then the head of the house must lead off, not in lordliness, but by humbling himself, begging forgiveness for whatever may have been wrong in his attitude, conduct, or behavior. This will spell death to any bullheadedness on the part of the head. It does not matter whether or not she was the guiltier party in the domestic difference. Husband, with no stipulations on your part you are to love your wife as Christ loved the church and gave Himself for her life. This is God's call to every Christian husband.

In Colossians 3:19 Paul points out a common fault among husbands—*harshness*. "Husbands, love your wives and do not be harsh with them" (NIV). Harshness is first chilling, then killing—killing to the most promising marriage. The husband is to love his wife even unto self-sacrifice, with energy, purity, and constancy.

The gateway to all blessing is through the death-dealing doorway of repentance. Are you a Christian husband and therefore head of your home? As a godly spiritual head, you must be the first to repent. Let the head take the lead. Die head down; it will spell death to your ego. God's way up is down. "If any one wants to be first, he shall be last of all, and servant of all" (Mark 9:35, NASB). Thereby "we are to grow up in all aspects into Him, who is the head, even Christ" (Eph. 4:15, NASB).

In the closing chapter of Peter's first epistle we find God's plan for blessed harmony in the home. The secret is this: "Yea, all of you be subject one to another" (1 Peter 5:5). The wife is to be subject to the husband in affection, respect, and loyalty; and the husband is to be servant to the wife in self-sacrificing love and concern. Only thus can God's ideal for the home be attained; only thus can the home be a worthy portrayal of heaven itself, with Christ as the true Head.

Chapter Sixteen

LIBERTY AND RESPONSIBILITY

D avid the psalmist makes reference to women's twofold ministry—publishing the Word and ministering in the home. "The Lord giveth the word: the women that publish the tidings are a great host. Kings of armies flee, they flee; and she that tarrieth at home divideth the spoil" (Ps. 68:11-12, ASV). True liberty involves responsibility—God sets us free to do what we ought to do. Woman's true liberty allows her to be what God meant her to be and to do what God wills her to do.

Some women publish the tidings abroad; others serve mainly in the home; then there are those who fill both roles. Certain ladies seem to be specially endowed for public service, while others stay "by the stuff" (1 Sam. 30:24). Obviously God calls some to public ministry, but at the same time blesses those who stay at home in His will.

Throughout this book we have sought to emphasize that while God does not usually choose women for public positions, yet at times in His sovereignty He does so, especially when men do not shoulder their responsibilities. That God does choose to call and qualify some women for positions of leadership is proof that women are not intrinsically debarred from such offices because of their womanhood.

However, only a small minority of women are likely to function as pastors in the official sense, for the same reason that fewer women than men ever hold public office and serve as executive heads of great business concerns. Even in those denominations and fellowships where every official barrier against the recognition of women as ministers has been removed, not many women have taken advantage of the liberty thus afforded them.

Mrs. Dorothy Pape, a mother with a public ministry, writes,

> I do not see how a mother with children, or even most wives, could give their time to the twenty-four-hour-a-day duty expected of most ministers. On the other hand, I cannot find in Scripture that that is necessarily the church pattern God had in mind. If a woman has clear assurance of God's leading and no desire to "lord it over" anyone, it seems difficult to deny the validity of an audible ministry for her in Christian gatherings and in personal witness, since God Himself has chosen to use many women in this way.[1]

The home is doubtless the main realm of service for most of the Lord's handmaidens. Their chief function will ever be in connection with the home and the rearing of a family; but what greater privilege can be afforded a woman than the opportunity to nurture and lead her children in the way of righteousness? By example and precept she can be preparing them to fill some of the gaps in the harvest fields of the world.

Along with her home duties a mother can often reach out into other areas of Christian service without neglecting the family. How about the ministry of prayer, of hospitality, of encouragement by correspondence or telephone, and of sewing for the needy? Many a Dorcas has done noble work with her needle.

Essential to the sending forth of missionaries is a home base committed to their support. Without the loving labor and sacrificial service of those whom God leads to "hold the ropes" at home, the sent ones would lack adequate support in prayer and finances. The dedicated Christian mother, therefore, can be a vital link in the missionary chain: she can keep the home fires burning and at the same time participate in supportive missionary enterprise.

In *The New Acts of the Apostles* Dr. A.T. Pierson clearly shows the blessed balance between these two aspects of woman's service.

> Woman goes abroad as teacher, nurse and medical missionary, and in endurance and endeavor rivals the most patient and valiant; or as wife and mother, shows what Christ makes of her sex; and not only joins her husband in work, but sometimes equals and even outdoes him in service. One-third of the unevangelized can best be reached by women, and a large part of them can be reached by her only as they are inaccessible to man.[2]

The command to all disciples is, "Go ye therefore into all the world and preach the gospel to every creature." We have no command, "Stay at home." Every child of God must decide God's will for himself or herself—whether to stay at home or to go out publishing the Word. God will answer the seeking soul who wants to know His will in order to fulfill it. The promise is that those who tarry at home in the good and acceptable will of God shall surely share in the spoil with those who go out to the missionary front.

Woman's Liberation

Dr. J.G. Morrison aptly relates woman's liberation through the Gospel to her responsibility to exercise her gifts in Christian ministry, and he makes a stirring appeal to liberated women to lead the way in devoted service and sacrifice for the Lord Jesus Christ who has freed them from bondage.

The advent of Jesus Christ saved womanhood. Not only saved souls of those who accepted and believed on Him, but brought the whole human race to see, at least wherever the gospel light has spread at all, that woman's place is not at man's feet, but is at his side. . . .

[Christian] women, do not forget your heritage. You are the spiritual descendants of the Sarahs, the Deborahs, and the Hannahs of the Old Covenant. Your line is renewed again in the New Testament in Mary who gave birth to Jesus Christ; Elizabeth who mothered His great forerunner; in Mary of Bethany, who anointed His precious head and feet; in Mary Magdalene, who was last at His cross and first at His empty tomb; in the host of women who in early gospel days, gave their hearts, homes, and deepest toil to the cause of the Master. Your line is again renewed in church history, until for faithfulness, devotion, heroism, martyrdom and all else that pleases the heart of the great Christ, woman has led the way, borne the brunt, shared the vigils, preached with life and lip, and handed the cause on to the next age with its banners proudly breasting every gale of opposition! . . . Remember then, sisters, your marvelous heritage, and your amazing responsibility.[3]

May Dr. Morrison's challenge strike a responsive chord in every Christian woman's heart. As the Gospel has brought to woman glorious freedom from slavery and degradation, and has brought her true liberty to be all she was created to be, let her fulfill her calling. It is her supreme privilege as a creature made in God's image to show forth the otherwise invisible God in her appointed sphere in life, on the one hand unhampered by legalistic restrictions and on the other hand free from presumptuous or self-seeking ambition. Only then can she be satisfied and joyful in heart; only then can her life issue in rivers of blessing to the glory of God.

Bibliography

The Ante-Nicene Fathers. Ed. Alexander Roberts and James Donaldson. American ed. 12 vols. Grand Rapids: Eerdmans, repr. 1951.

Ayer, Henry Ward. *God's Ideal Woman*. New York: Calvary Baptist Church sermon booklet, January 10, 1937.

Baldwin, Ethel May and David V. Benson. *Henrietta Mears and How She Did It*. Ventura, California: Regal, 1966.

Barclay, William. *The Letters to Timothy, Titus and Philemon*. 2nd ed. Philadephia: The Westminster Press, 1960.

Bingham, Helen E. *An Irish Saint*. 19th ed. Jamestown, NC: Newby, 1927.

Blackwelder, Boyce W. *Light from the Greek New Testament*. Grand Rapids: Baker, 1958.

Boldrey, Richard and Joyce. *Chauvinist or Feminist? (Paul's View of Women)*. Grand Rapids: Baker, 1972.

Boom, Corrie ten. *Plenty for Everyone*. Fort Washington, Penn.: Christian Literature Crusade, 1967.

Booth, Catherine. *Female Ministry*. 1859; New York: Salvation Army Supplies Printing, 1975.

Bruce, F.F. *The Acts of the Apostles, Greek Text*. Grand Rapids: Eerdmans, 1951.

Burgess, Alan. *The Small Woman*. London: Bell & Hyman, 1957.

Bushnell, Katherine C. *God's Word to Women*. 4th ed. Corona, Calif.; Scripture Studies Concern, 1930.

Chilvers, Ethel E. *The Ministry of Women*. London: Stanley Martin, 1923.

Clarke, Adam. *The Holy Bible containing the Old and New Testaments with a Commentary and Critical Notes.* 6 vols. New York: Abingdon-Cokesbury, n.d.

Conybeare, W.J. and J.S. Howson. *The Life and Epistles of St. Paul.* Grand Rapids: Eerdmans, repr. 1968.

Denney, James. The Second Epistle to the Corinthians, *The Expositor's Bible.* Ed. W. Robertson Nicoll. New York: Funk & Wagnalls, 1900.

DuBose, Hampden C. *The Dragon, Image, and Demon.* New York: Armstrong, 1887.

Edersheim, Alfred. *Sketches of Jewish Social Life (in the Days of Christ).* 1876; Grand Rapids: Eerdmans, 1980.

Ellicott, Charles John. Ed. *An Old and New Testament Commentary for English Readers.* 8 vols. London: Cassell, 1897. Exodus by George Rawlinson.

Exell, Joseph S. Ed. *The Biblical Illustrator.* 1 Corinthians, quoting Marcus Dods. Grand Rapids: Baker, 1958.

Fairbairn, Patrick. *Commentary on the Pastoral Epistles.* 1874; Grand Rapids: Zondervan, 1956.

Fitzwater, P.B. *Woman (Her Mission, Position, and Ministry).* Grand Rapids: Eerdmans, 1949.

Foster, Elon. *New Cyclopaedia of Illustrations.* New York: Palmer, 1872.

Garrard, Mary N. *Mrs. Penn-Lewis, A Memoir.* Poole, England: The Overcomer Literature Trust, 1930.

Glover, Robert Hall. *The Progress of World-Wide Missions.* 4th ed. 1924; Harper, 1953.

Godet, F. *The Gospel of Luke.* 2 vols. Edinburgh: T. & T. Clark, 1878, I.

Gordon, Ernest. *A Book of Protestant Saints.* Rev. and enlarged. Chicago: Moody, 1946.

Hastings, Edward and James. Eds. *The Speaker's Bible.* The First Epistle to the Corinthians. 2 vols. 1927; Grand Rapids: Baker, 1962, II.

Henry, Matthew. *An Exposition of the Old and New Testaments.* 6 vols. New ed., rev. New York: Revell, n.d.

Hitt, Russell T. *Sensei (The Life Story of Irene Webster-Smith).* New York: Harper & Row, 1965.

Hodge, Charles. *An Exposition of the First Epistle to the Corinthians.* Grand Rapids: Eerdmans, 1959.

Jamieson, Robert, A.R. Fausset, David Brown. *A Commentary on the Old and New Testaments*. 6 vols. Grand Rapids: Eerdmans, 1945.

Judd, C.H. *Woman's Place in the Church, as Taught in Holy Scripture*. Glasgow: The Scottish Bible and Book Society, n.d.

Keil, C.F. and F. Delitzsch. *Biblical Commentary on the Old Testament*. The Pentateuch by Delitzsch. Grand Rapids: Eerdmans, 1949, I.

The Koran. Transl. from Arabic by J.M. Rodwell. London: J.M. Dent, Everyman's Library, 1909.

Lang, G.H. *The Churches of God*. London: C.J. Thynne & Jarvis, 1928.

Lange, John Peter. *A Commentary on the Holy Scriptures*. New York: Charles Scribner, 1868.

Liddell, Henry George and Robert Scott. *A Greek-English Lexicon*. Rev. and augmented by Sir Henry Stuart Jones. 1843; Oxford: Clarendon Press, 1968.

Lightfoot, J.B. *The Epistle of St. Paul to the Galatians*. Grand Rapids: Zondervan, 1957.

Lockyer, Herbert. *The Women of the Bible*. Grand Rapids: Zondervan, 1967.

Lyall, Leslie T. Historical Prelude, *The Awakening* by Marie Monsen. London: China Inland Mission, 1961.

McClintock, John and James Strong. *Cyclopaedia of Biblical, Theological, and Ecclesiastical Literature*. 12 vols. 1867-1887; Grand Rapids: Baker, 1981, V. Article on "Marriage."

Meyer, F.B. *The Epistle to the Philippians*. London: The Religious Tract Society, n.d.

Millar, J.P. *Judges* in *The Preacher's Complete Homiletic Commentary on the Old Testament* by various authors. 21 vols. New York: Funk & Wagnalls, n.d.

Milne, Bruce. *Know the Truth*. Downers Grove, Illinois: InterVarsity, 1982.

Morrison, J.G. *Satan's Subtle Attack on Woman*. Kansas City, Missouri: Nazarene Publishing House, n.d.

Needham, Mrs. George C. *Woman's Ministry*. New York: Charles C. Cook, n.d.

Newell, William R. *Romans*. Chicago: Moody, 1938.

Nilsen, Maria and Paul H. Sheetz. *Malla Moe*. Chicago: Moody, 1956.

Orr, James. Ed. *The International Standard Bible Encyclopedia*. 6 vols. Grand

Rapids: Eerdmans, 1939, V, article on "Woman," by Dwight M. Pratt.

Pape, Dorothy R. *In Search of God's Ideal Woman*. Downers Grove, Illinois: InterVarsity, 1976.

Penn-Lewis, Mrs. Jessie. *The "Magna Charta" of Woman "According to the Scriptures,"* 3rd ed. Poole, England: Overcomer Literature Trust, 1948.

Pierson, Arthur T. *The Bible and Spiritual Life*. London: James Nisbet, 1908.

_____ *The New Acts of the Apostles*. New York: Baker & Taylor, 1894.

Pitman, E.R. *Lady Missionaries in Many Lands*. Basingstoke, England: Marshall Pickering, n.d.

Ryle, John Charles. *Expository Thoughts on the Gospel of St. Luke*. 2 vols. London: Hodder & Stoughton, MCMX.

_____ *Expository Thoughts on the Gospels*, St. Mark. London: Hodder & Stoughton, MCMX.

Stalker, James. *The Trial and Death of Jesus Christ*. New York: Doubleday, Doran, 1929.

Stockton, Amy Lee. *The Word of the Woman*. U.S.A.: Stockton and Gould, 1956.

Strahan, James. *The Maréchale*. 8th ed. New York: George H. Doran, 1921.

Strong, Augustus Hopkins. *Systematic Theology*. 11th ed. Philadelphia: Judson, 1947.

Thomas, W.H. Griffith. *Outline Studies in the Gospel of Luke*. Grand Rapids: Eerdmans, 1950.

Titterton, C.T. *Five Great Non-Christian Religions*. London: The Inter-Varsity Fellowship of Evangelical Unions, 1936.

Trapp, John. *A Commentary on the Old and New Testaments*. Ed. W. Webster. 5 vols. London: Richard Dickinson, 1868, II.

Upham, Thomas C. *Life of Madame Guyon*. London: Allenson, reprint 1908.

Vaughan, Louisa. *Answered or Unanswered? (Miracles of Faith in China)*. 1917; Philadelphia: Christian Life Literature Fund, rev. and enlarged 1920. Reprinted by Prairie Press, Three Hills, Alberta under title, *The Work of Faith with Power*, 1965.

Williams, George. *The Student's Commentary on the Holy Scriptures*. 5th ed. 1926; Basingstoke, England: Marshall Pickering, 1949.

Zwemer, Dr. and Mrs. Samuel M. *Moslem Women*. North Cambridge, Mass.: The Central Committee on the United Study of Foreign Mission, 1926.

Articles and Periodicals

Farham, Myrnia F. "The Ideal of Womanhood." *Dawn*. London: Vol. 26, March 1948.

Fellman, "Emma Dryer: Visionary of a Bible School." *Moody Monthly*, May 1985.

Frederick, Edward L. "Are the Heathen Lost?" *The Eastern Challenge*. International Missions, Wayne, N.J., date unknown.

Frame, Raymond. "Commit to Faithful Women." *E.M.F. Reporter*, date unknown.

Gordon, A.J. "The Ministry of Women." *The Alliance Weekly*, December 8, 1928 and December 15, 1928.

Guinness, Mrs. Grattan. "The Ministry of Women." *The Prairie Overcomer*, vol. 39, April 1966.

Hardesty, Nancy. "Great Women of Faith." *Eternity*, May 1975.

Kligerman, Aaron Judah. "Christ and the Womanhood of the World." *Good News Broadcaster*, Lincoln, Neb., October, 1968.

MacLean, B. Hutmacher. "Ingrid Webber's mission is a celebration of life." *Wenatchee World* (Wenatchee, Wash.), November 15, 1981.

Miller, Dorothy Ruth. "On Women Speaking." *The Prairie Pastor*, Three Hills, Alberta, Vol. 12, December, 1939.

Pratt, Dwight M. "Women." *The International Bible Encyclopedia*. Ed. James Orr. 6 vols. Grand Rapids: Eerdmans, 1939, V.

Slessor, Mary. "Devotional (Prayer)." *Dawn*. London, vol. XXVIII, October 1950.

Wall, Gary L. with Dave Raney and Kay Oliver. "The Equal Rights Amendment." *Moody Monthly*, November 1978.

Wall, Gary L. "Dialogue with Phyllis Schlafly." *Moody Monthly*, November 1978.

Young, Esther. "Paganism and Womanhood." *Dawn*, London, vol. XXVIII, March 1950.

Unpublished Material

Hancock, Maxine. Personal letter.

Humble Disciple, A. *The Ministry of Women.* An unpublished manuscript by a writer who calls himself "a humble disciple."

The Ministry of Women. Unpublished manuscript of Salvation Army Principles. November 26, 1977.

Notes

CHAPTER ONE. WHAT DOES THE SCRIPTURE SAY?

1. Mrs. George C. Needham, *Women's Ministry* (New York: Charles C. Cook, n.d.), p. 5.

2. Edward and James Hastings, eds. *The Speaker's Bible, The First Epistle to the Corinthians*, 2 vols. (1927; Grand Rapids: Baker, 1962), II, p. 112.

3. E.R. Pitman, *Lady Missionaries in Many Lands* (Basingstoke, England: Marshall Pickering, n.d.), pp. 6–7. Used by permission.

4. A.J. Gordon, "The Ministry of Women," *The Alliance Weekly*, December 8, 1928. Used by permission.

CHAPTER TWO. LEARNING FROM HEBREW HISTORY

1. George Rawlinson, Exodus, *An Old and New Testament Commentary for English Readers*, ed. Charles John Ellicot, 8 vols. (London: Cassell, 1897), I, p. 244.

2. G.H. Lang, *The Churches of God* (London: C.J. Thyme and Jarvis, 1928), p. 80.

3. Ethel E. Chilvers, *The Ministry of Women* (London: Stanley Martin, 1923), p. 26.

4. F.W. Farrar, Judges, *An Old and New Testament Commentary for English Readers*, II, p. 195.

5. Herbert Lockyer, *The Women of the Bible* (Grand Rapids, Zondervan, 1967), p. 66.

6. Matthew Henry, *An Exposition of the Old and New Testaments*, 6 vols. (new ed., rev.; New York: Revell, n.d.), II, on 2 Kings 22.

7. Adam Clarke, *The Holy Bible containing the Old and New Testaments with a Commentary and Critical Notes*, 6 vols. (New York: Abingdon-Cokesbury, n.d.), III, p. 432 on Psalm 68:11.

8. *Ibid.*, IV, p. 160 on Isaiah 40:9.

9. Lang, p. 85.

CHAPTER THREE. WOMAN AT CREATION AND AFTER THE FALL

1. P.B. Fitzwater, *Woman (Her Mission, Position, and Ministry)* (Grand Rapids: Eerdmans, 1949), p. 27.

2. Arthur T. Pierson, *The Bible and Spiritual Life* (London: James Nisbet, 1908), pp. 57–58.

3. F. Delitzsch, *The Pentateuch, in Biblical Commentary on the Old Testament* by C.F. Keil and F. Delitzsch, trans. from German by James Martin, 3 vols. (Grand Rapids: Eerdmans, 1949), I, p,. 86.

4. Matthew Henry, I, on Genesis 2.

5. Fitzwater, p. 27.

6. Bruce Milne, *Know the Truth* (Downers Grove, Illinois: Inter-Varsity, 1982), p. 99.

7. Pierson, *The Bible and Spiritual Life*, pp. 58–59.

8. Henry Ward Ayer, *God's Ideal Woman* (New York: Calvary Baptist Church sermon booklet, January 10, 1937), p. 6.

9. Pierson, *The Bible and Spiritual Life*, p. 59.

10. *Ibid.*, pp. 67–68.

11. John Peter Lange, *A Commentary on the Holy Scriptures* (New York:

Charles Scribner, 1868), I, p. 225.

12. Katharine C. Bushnell, *God's Word to Women*, (4th ed.; Corona Calif.: Scripture Studies Concern, 1930), paragraphs 130, 139.

13. *Ibid.*, para. 137, quoting Mitchell in *The World Before Abraham*.

14. *Ibid.*, para. 132.

15. Dorothy R. Pape, *In Search of God's Ideal Woman* (Downers Grove, Ill.: InterVarsity Press, 1976), p. 192. Used by permission.

16. Bushnell, para. 243.

17. Alfred Edersheim. *Sketches of Jewish Social Life (in the Days of Christ)* (1876; Grand Rapids: Eerdmans, 1980), p. 154.

18. Tertullian, "On the Apparel of Women," written about A.D. 202, De Cultu Feminarum I, 1, in *The Ante-Nicene Fathers*, ed. Alexander Roberts and James Donaldson, transl. 1867 Edinburgh ed., American ed., 10 vols. (Grand Rapids: Eerdmans, 1951), IV, p. 14.

19. Mrs. Jessie Penn-Lewis, *The "Magna Charta" of Woman "According to the Scriptures"* (3rd ed.; Poole, England: The Overcomer Literature Trust, 1948), p. 25. Used by permission.

CHAPTER FOUR. MALE AND FEMALE DISTINCTIVES

1. Fitzwater, p. 31.

2. Gary L. Wall with Dave Raney and Kay Oliver, "The Equal Rights Amendment," *Moody Monthly*, November 1978, pp. 40–42.

3. Wall, "Dialogue with Phyllis Schafly," *Moody Monthly*, November 1978, p. 47.

4. James Denney, *The Second Epistle to the Corinthians*, in *The Expositor's Bible*, ed. W. Robertson Nicoll (New York: Funk & Wagnalls, 1900), pp. 315–316.

5. G.H. Lang, p. 84.

6. Clarke, VI, p. 503 on 1 Timothy 2:13.

7. *Ibid.*, p. 858 on 1 Peter 3:7.

8. *Ibid.*

9. Pape, p. 293.

10. Lange, IX of the N.T., The Epistles General of Peter, p. 54, quoting Martin Luther.

11. *Ibid.*, pp. 53–54.

12. *Ibid.*, p. 54.

13. Patrick Fairbairn, *Commentary on the Pastoral Epistles* (1874; Grand Rapids: Zondervan, 1956), p. 129.

14. J.G. Morrison, *Satan's Subtle Attack on Woman* (Kansas City, Missouri: Nazarene Publishing House, n.d.), p. 9.

CHAPTER FIVE. MINISTERING WOMEN IN THE GOSPELS.

1. Arthur T. Pierson, *The New Acts of the Apostles* (New York: Baker & Taylor, 1894), p. 133.

2. Lockyer, p. 93.

3. F. Godet, *The Gospel of Luke*, 2 vols. (Edinburgh: T. & T. Clark, 1878), I, p. 144.

4. David Brown, *A Commentary on the Old and New Testaments*, 6 vols., by Jamieson, Fausset, and Brown (Grand Rapids: Eerdmans, 1945), V, quoting Alford, p, 251.

5. A writer who calls himself "A humble disciple," in an unpublished manuscript, *The Ministry of Women*, p. 11.

6. Lockyer, p. 237.

7. John Charles Ryle, *Expository Thoughts on the Gospel of St. Luke*, 2 vols. (London: Hodder & Stoughton, MCMX), I, pp. 244–245.

8. James Stalker, *The Trial and Death of Jesus Christ* (Garden City, NY: Doubleday, Doran, 1894), pp. 146–147.

9. *Ibid.*, p. 152.

10. *Ibid.*, pp. 147–148.

11. J.C. Ryle, *Expository Thoughts on the Gospels, St. Mark* (London: Hodder & Stoughton, MCMX), p. 350.

12. Ryle, *St. Luke*, I, p. 245.

13. Catherine Booth, *Female Ministry* (1859; New York: Salvation Army Supplies Printing & Publishing Dept., 1975), p. 16. Used by permission.

CHAPTER SIX. WOMEN OF THE EARLY CHURCH

1. F.F. Bruce, *The Acts of the Apostles*, Greek Text (Grand Rapids: Eerdmans, 1951), p. 74.

2. *Ibid.*

3. Pitman, pp. 9–10.

4. Dwight M. Pratt, "Women," *The International Standard Bible Encyclopedia*, ed. James Orr, 6 vols. (Grand Rapids: Eerdmans, 1939), V, p. 3103.

5. Brown, VI on Acts, p. 115.

6. Chilvers, p. 37.

7. A humble disciple, p. 15 quoting Papias.

8. Clarke, VI on Acts, p. 858.

9. William R. Newell, *Romans* (Chicago: Moody Press, 1938), p. 551 footnote. (Originally published by Grace Publications, Chicago.)

10. A.J. Gordon, "The Ministry of Women," *The Alliance Weekly*, December 15, 1928. Used by permission.

11. A humble disciple, p. 27, quoting Bishop Lightfoot in *Primary Charge*, p. 33.

12. Bushnell, para. 364.

13. Pape, p. 213 quoting Pliny.

14. H.D.M. Spence, 1 Timothy in *An Old and New Testament Commentary for English Readers*, VIII, p. 193.

15. Henry George Liddell and Robert Scott, *A Greek-English Lexicon*, rev. and augmented by Sir Henry Stuart Jones (1843; Oxford: Clarendon Press, 1968), p. 1526.

16. Pape, p. 210.

17. W.J. Conybeare and J.S. Howson, *The Life and Epistles of St. Paul* (Grand Rapids: Eerdmans, rep. 1968), p. 497.

18. Pape, p. 209.

19. Lange, V of the New Testament on Romans, p. 447.

20. Adolf Von Harnack, quoted by Pape, p. 215.

21. A humble disciple, quoting Chrysostom, p. 28.

22. F.B. Meyer, *The Epistle to the Philippians* (London: The Religious Tract Society, n.d.), p, 213.

CHAPTER SEVEN. "NO MALE AND FEMALE"

1. William Barclay, *The Letters to Timothy, Titus and Philemon* (2nd ed.; Philadelphia: The Westminster Press, 1960), p. 77.

2. Hastings, *The Speaker's Bible, The First Epistle to the Corinthians*, II, p. 112.

3. Boldreys, p. 33.

4. A.R. Fausset, *A Commentary on the Old and New Testaments*, 6 vols., by Jamieson, Fausset, and Brown, 1945), VI, Galatians, p. 358.

5. Richard and Joyce Boldrey, *Chauvinist or Feminist? (Paul's View of Women)* (Grand Rapids: Baker, 1972) pp. 33, 46.

6. Aaron Judah Klingerman, "Christ and the Womanhood of the World," *Good News Broadcaster*, October 1968.

CHAPTER EIGHT. WOMEN'S RIGHT TO PROPHESY.

1. A.J. Gordon, "The Ministry of Women," *The Alliance Weekly*, December 8, 1828, quoting Hackett on Acts, p. 49.

2. Clarke, VI, p. 250 on 1 Corinthians 11:5.

3. *The Ministry of Women*, unpublished manuscript of Salvation Army Principles, November 26, 1977, p. 1.

4. Joseph S. Exell, *The Biblical Illustrator* (Grand Rapids: Baker, 1958), vol. II on 1 Corinthians, quoting Marcus Dods, p. 81.

5. Hastings, The First Epistle to the Corinthians, II, p. 111.

6. Exell, 1 Corinthians, II, quoting Marcus Dods, p. 81.

7. *Ibid*.

8. A humble disciple, p. 20.

9. *Ibid*., quoting Bishop Lightfoot, p. 17.

10. Bushnell, para. 243.

11. Clarke, VI, on 1 Corinthians, p. 250.

12. Charles Hodge, *An Exposition of the First Epistle to the Corinthians* (Grand Rapids: Eerdmans, 1959), pp. 204–205.

13. *Ibid*., p. 212.

14. James Strahan, *The Maréchale* (8th ed.; New York: George H. Doran, 1921), p. 146.

15. J.B. Lightfoot, *The Epistle of St. Paul to the Galatians* (Grand Rapids: Zondervan, 1957), p. 150.

CHAPTER NINE. HARMONIZING 1 CORINTHIANS 11 AND 14

1. C.F. Hogg, The Ministry of Women, p. 13, quoted by a humble disciple, p. 16.

2. A humble disciple, p. 20.

3. Boyce W. Blackwelder, *Light from the Greek New Testament* (Grand Rapids: Baker, 1958), pp. 55-57. Used by permission.

4. Lang, pp. 75–76.

5. Strong, pp. 546–547.

6. Needham, pp. 48–49.

CHAPTER TEN. SILENCE FOR WOMEN?

1. A.J. Gordon, "The Ministry of Women," *The Alliance Weekly*, December 8, 1928.

2. William Ramsey in *The Expositor*, September, 1909, quoted by a humble disciple, p. 24.

3. F.F. Bruce in *The Harvester*, answer to question 1,038, quoted by a humble disciple, p. 24.

4. A humble disciple, p. 25.

5. Booth, p. 13.

6. A humble disciple, p. 25.

7. George Williams, *The Student's Commentary on the Holy Scriptures* (1926; 5th ed.; Basingstoke, England: Marshall Pickering, 1949) p. 954.

8. J.H. Robinson, quoted by Booth, p. 12.

9. Amy Lee Stockton, *The Word of the Woman* (USA: Stockton and Gould, 1956), p. 16.

10. J.H. Robinson, quoted by Booth, pp. 12–13.

11. Dr. Taft quoted by Booth, p. 13.

12. A humble disciple, p. 26.

13. D. Edmond Hiebert, "The Apostle Paul: Women's Friend," in *The Christian Reader*, June-July 1973) quoted by Pape, p. 150.

14. C.H. Judd of the China Inland Mission, *Woman's Place in the*

Church, as Taught in Holy Scripture (Glasgow: The Scottish Bible and Book Society, n.d.), p. 11.

15. Pape, p. 233.

16. Needham, pp. 43–44.

17. Augustus Hopkins Strong, *Systematic Theology* (11th ed.; Philadelphia: Judson, 1947), p. 546.

18. F.F. Bruce as quoted by a humble disciple, p. 23.

19. Stockton, p. 3.

CHAPTER ELEVEN. GLIMPSES INTO CHURCH HISTORY

1. Pape, p. 224.

2. Pratt, p. 3104.

3. Pitman, p. 10.

4. Jonathan Blanchard, quoted by Pape, p. 228.

5. Source unknown.

6. A.J. Gordon, "The Ministry of Women," *The Alliance Weekly*, December 15, 1928.

7. Penn-Lewis, pp. 42–43.

CHAPTER TWELVE. MINISTERING WOMEN IN OUR WESTERN WORLD

1. Corrie ten Boom, *Plenty for Everyone* (Fort Washington, Penn.: Christian Literature Crusade, 1967), pp. 66-68. Used by permission of CLC, Fort Washington, Penn.

2. Nancy Hardesty, "Great Women of Faith," *Eternity*, May 1975, on Catherine Booth, co-founder of Salvation Army. Reprinted by permission of *Eternity Magazine*, copyright 1975, Evangelical Ministries, Inc., 1716 Spruce Street, Philadelphia, Penn. 19103.

3. *Ibid.*

4. Strahan, p. 7.

5. *Ibid.*, p. 21.

6. *Ibid.*, p. 7.

7. *Ibid.*, pp. 254–255.

8. *The Ministry of Women*, unpublished manuscript of Salvation Army Principles, November 26, 1977, p. 1.

9. Mary N. Garrard, *Mrs. Penn-Lewis, A Memoir*, (Poole, England: The Overcomer Literature Trust, 1930), pp. 266, 269.

10. Ethel May Baldwin and David V. Benson, *Henrietta Mears and How She Did It* (Glendale, California, Regal, 1966), p. 143.

11. *Ibid.*, p. 142.

12. Eric Fellman, "Emma Dryer: Visionary of a Bible School," *Moody Monthly*, May 1985, p. 84.

13. *Ibid.*, p. 82.

14. *Ibid.*

15. *Ibid.*, p. 84.

16. Maxine Hancock, personal letter.

17. Dorothy Ruth Miller, "On Women Speaking," *The Prairie Pastor*, Three Hills, vol. 12, December, 1939.

18. Stockton, pp. 6–8.

19. *Ibid.*, p. 2.

CHAPTER THIRTEEN. WOMEN AND MISSIONS

1. Newell, p. 553 footnote.

2. Pitman, p. 17.

3. *Ibid.*, pp. 23–24.

4. Robert Hall Glover, *The Progress of World-Wide Missions* (1924; New York: Harper, 1953), p. 112.

5. *Ibid.* p. 114.

6. Louisa Vaughan, *Answered or Unanswered? (Miracles of Faith in China)* (1917; Philadelphia: Christian Life Literature Fund, rev. and enlarged 1920), pp. 12–13.

7. *Ibid.*, pp. 14–15.

8. Russell T. Hitt, *Sensei (The Life Story of Irene Webster-Smith)* (New York: Harper & Row, 1965), dust cover; see also pp. 203, 207, 209, 229.

9. Pape, p. 244.

10. Alan Burgess, *The Small Woman* (London: Bell & Hyman, 1957), pp. 189–190.

11. Booth, p. 18.

12. Glover, p. 250.

13. Mary Slessor in *Dawn*, vol. XXVIII, October 1950, p. 317, from *Living Links*.

14. Maria Nilsen and Paul H. Sheetz, *Malla Moe* (Chicago: Moody, 1956), p. 21.

15. *Ibid.*, pp. 25–26.

CHAPTER FOURTEEN. PERSISTENT PREJUDICE

1. A.J. Gordon, quoted by G.H. Lang, *The Churches of God*, pp. 86–87.

2. Booth, pp. 17–18.

3. Strahan, p. 143.

4. *Ibid.*, pp. 118–119.

5. *Ibid.*, p. 240.

6. *Ibid.*, p. 254.

7. Raymond Frame, "Commit to Faithful Women," *E.M.F. Reporter*, n.d.

8. B. Hutmacher MacLean, "Ingrid Webber's mission is a celebration of life," *Wenatchee World* (Wenatchee, Washington, Nov. 15, 1981) A3.

9. Mrs. Grattan Guinness, "The Ministry of Women," quoted in Memoir of Mrs. Henry Dening, *Prairie Overcomer* (vol. 39, April 1966), p. 130.

10. Lang, p. 86.

11. Pierson, *New Acts*, p. 386.

12. *Ibid.*, pp. 387–388.

13. J.P. Millar, *Judges* in *The Preacher's Complete Homiletic Commentary on the Old Testament* by various authors, 21 vols. (New York: Funk and Wagnalls, n.d.), p. 228.

14. Newell, *Romans*, p. 553 footnote.

15. Helen E. Bingham, *An Irish Saint* (19th ed.; Jamestown, N.C., Newby Book Room, 1927), p. 13.

CHAPTER SIXTEEN. LIBERTY AND RESPONSIBILITY

1. Pape, pp. 207–208.

2. Pierson, *New Acts*, p. 386.

3. Morrison, pp. 7, 22–23.